FOREWORD
STEPHANI B. CUDDIE, ED.D.

I was delighted to find out Scotty was writing a book and honored when he asked me to write the foreword. As a former student, Scotty always had a passion for writing that was apparent no matter what he was writing about or whom he was writing for.

My Conscious Endeavor is not a how-to book full of 'fluffy-bunny' rhetoric with steps to making a better life for yourself, but a real-life raw account of how Scotty came to be the man he is today, living his life each and every day with purpose and intention. While reading *My Conscious Endeavor* I laughed and cried, my heart broke for his struggles, and found joy in his triumph. I believe that Scotty wrote this book not in an attempt to make anyone feel sorry for him, but to share his story and let others know that ANYTHING is possible when you set about living your life as a conscious endeavor, no matter what curveballs life throws at you.

I believe this book will inspire others to live life as a conscious endeavor, to wake up each day and grab themselves by their bootstraps and overcome the obstacles placed in their path. If higher education is something you set your sights upon then be intentional about the pursuit, give it your all, be conscious in the process, because the rewards of higher education go beyond the degree and job prospects, higher education has the ability to be life-changing. As Henry David Thoreau wrote about students and the pursuit of higher education in *Walden*, "I mean that they should not play life, or study it merely, while the community supports them at this expensive game, but earnestly live it from beginning to end". I encourage you to live your life, making each day a conscious endeavor, no matter what you are doing.

Thank you, Scotty, for sharing the beginning of your amazing journey with us, for making the conscious endeavor to become who you are. It was my pleasure to be part of your academic endeavor and is my honor to be your friend.

My Conscious Endeavor

Scotty Rushing

ISBN: 1517538998
ISBN-13: 978-1517538996

DEDICATION

This book is dedicated to Loutheree Tompkins, my grandmother. Granny was a constant source of support and encouragement in my life. I hope that she is in a place where she can see what I am doing now and maybe even guide me a little as I continue my conscious endeavor.

CONTENTS

ACKNOWLEDGMENTS

This book would not have been published without the support and encouragement of so many wonderful people. It is impossible for me to mention them all but I would like to especially thank Sharon Soileau, Jeff and Lacie Burningham, Samer Kattouf, Ben Tuller, Laith Al Qasem, Ola Hamodi, Dr. Stephani Cuddie, Dr. Chuck Severance, and all of my former professors and classmates at the Florida Institute of Technology.

INTRODUCTION

The great irony of life is that it offers but one inevitability: death. The moment will come when life and all of the opportunities it offers are no more. The chance to create something of value, to do something meaningful with the life you've been given, is finite. There is no promise of tomorrow or next week or next year, or even the time it will take you to read this book.

Your only guarantee is right now.

The Bible speaks about a man named Methuselah. You are probably familiar with the name because it has become synonymous with a person that is very old. Methuselah is said to have lived to be 969 years old, quite an accomplishment when you consider that he existed in an age without chiropractors, wonder diets, or medical marijuana. Bear in mind that Methuselah was also quite…virile. He had many sons and daughters. Any parent will tell you that worry shortens the lifespan and lengthens the gray hairs. If Methuselah had been childless he might have survived to edit this book.

Stories like that of Methuselah are hard to swallow as fact, of course, but legends are steeped in truth. I started to think about Methuselah one day and look for the truth inside the myth. What if the length of a man's life was reckoned not only by how long he physically lived but by how long he was remembered after his death? Let's theorize that Methuselah physically lived to be 70 and was remembered by future generations for another 899 years. What kind of life must Methuselah have lived in order for his memory to endure so long?

Let me put this in perspective. Ask yourself if you remember these three individuals and their accomplishments. Be honest! No Googling! Ready?

Philo Farnsworth. Roger Sherman. Sybil Ludington.

How many did you get? I'm going to guess that most individuals would have a hard time remembering any of these people or what they achieved. Don't feel bad. I had to research them as my examples.

Philo Farnsworth lived from 1906 until 1971. He was an inventor who created an "image dissector" that was critical to the development of electronic television sets. Roger Sherman lived from 1721 until 1793 and was a Founding Father of the United States. He is the only person to sign all four of America's founding documents: the Continental Association, the Declaration of Independence, the Articles of Confederation, and the Constitution. Sybil Ludington lived from 1761 until 1839 and was a heroine of the Revolutionary War. On April 26, 1777, a 16-year old Sybil mounted her horse Star for a midnight ride that was twice the distance of the famous one taken by Paul Revere so that she could alert the colonial forces to the approach of the British.

Farnsworth, Sherman, and Ludington accomplished some monumental things that literally helped to shape the world as we know it today, yet all three and their achievements are mostly forgotten. Can you even imagine what Methuselah must have accomplished to have been remembered by future generations for 969 years in a time when there were no written records and no Internet? Word of mouth kept this man's legacy alive for almost a millennium.

We arrive now at the all-important question.

How long will the world remember you after you're gone?

In 2005 a chain of events began that motivated me in a painful and powerful way to consider the value I was creating with my own life. I was 37 years old, divorced, and attempting to raise a 13 year-old daughter by myself. I had a job I'd held for several years that barely paid the bills. My possessions were meager. Aside from my beautiful, smart, sweet-spirited daughter there was little I could take pride in where my life was concerned. I'd been offered a band scholarship to the University of Texas as I prepared to graduate from Hawkins High School but turned it down, reasoning that I did not want to spend another four years giving up my fall weekends marching with the college band at football games. What I really wanted to do was be a writer. I'd shown some flashes of talent, but my work ethic was dreadful. The years piled up and time did what time does: it seduced me into thinking that there were an unlimited number of days to discover my purpose and carve my personal legacy.

Sometimes life has to hit us pretty hard in order to break the siren-like spell of time and force us to face the reality that our days are numbered. For me, the blows were severe. I lost my steady job, became homeless, and was dealt a health crisis that made me keenly aware of how important it is to celebrate each moment as a unique opportunity for growth and change. Today, I can embrace my hardships because they led me to a place of understanding and purpose.

Several years ago I adopted a quote from Henry David Thoreau as my personal motto. In *Walden*, Thoreau writes:

"I know of no more encouraging fact than the unquestionable ability of man to elevate his life by a conscious endeavor."

Those words became my catalyst for change. In that one sentence I found hope, hope that no matter what my circumstances I could sculpt the clay of my existence into a joyful and fulfilling life. I found faith in my ability to harness inner resources I didn't realize I had. I found a new understanding of how a person's character is refined through hardship. As you read this book I want to challenge you to seize the encouragement Thoreau speaks of and think about the endeavor you are making to improve your own quality of life. I would submit to you that your potential is limitless if you will only harness the inner resources that all men and women possess. You are much stronger than you think. Your life can begin to change and take a new direction immediately if you seize the power of a conscious endeavor. It doesn't matter how old you are, how much money you have or don't have, or how great your challenges seem to be. The ability to create a lasting legacy is within your grasp.

I believe in the power of a conscious endeavor.

I believe in *you*.

Scotty Rushing
Hall Summit, LA
September 2015

PART ONE:
QUIET DESPERATION

"The mass of men lead lives of quiet desperation."
Henry David Thoreau, *Walden*

1 FALSE NOBILITY

A concept that rests at the heart of the American Dream is that there is nobility in working hard. I think that's true with one important qualification. There is nobility in working hard *with purpose*.

My mother had a reputation as a hard worker. She was a single mom and working was a necessity. My absent father did not pay child support and my mother never received government assistance. Her jobs were menial, most of them in the food service industry. She never earned much more than minimum wage. There was little purpose driving my mother's life beyond earning enough money to pay the rent and keep the lights on. We never had much more than the basic necessities. I had a sweet and loving grandmother that did so much to fill my life with the things my mother wasn't equipped to provide, including profound love and encouragement.

Hers is a tale that is all too common in the world today. My mother became pregnant out of wedlock, got married because she understood the stigma an unwed mother must face, and soon after she gave birth assumed the responsibility of raising a child by herself. I came into the world on the evening of October 15, 1967 with a headful of thick hair that befitted the times. It was the end of the Summer of Love in a very literal sense; my father exited my life just eighteen months later. I saw him once after that but my memory of his visit is almost nonexistent.

My mother remarried a good man when I was seven years old and he made every effort to be an excellent role model for me and treat me like a son. He was quite older than my mom and had no children of his own. We lived together on a 138-acre farm just outside of Tyler, Texas in a small community called Red Springs. I didn't know it or appreciate it then but this was as close as I was ever going to come to an idyllic upbringing.

There were problems that plagued my mother throughout her life. The biggest of these was alcoholism. My mother was a fierce alcoholic that had spent most of her young adulthood in the rough bars and honkytonks of Texas. She lived in Dallas for a time and claimed to have frequented Jack Ruby's nightclubs. I can remember a picture of her taken in a Ft. Worth ballroom. She was dressed in the gaudy Texas chic that was the preferred garb of barflies and appeared to be having the time of her life. I believe she was. Her adventures brought her into contact with some of the biggest country music stars of the era including Ray Price and Tony Douglas. It was a fast life for a girl that in all likelihood was unprepared to have the brakes applied by the arrival of a child.

My mother and I had a strained relationship at best and I have always believed this was due, at least in part, to a lingering resentment. She was 30 when I came along and I believe that my mother would have been very happy to remain childless. I was an accident—there can be little doubt of this—and my arrival threatened her party lifestyle. Even after I was born she did not willingly give up her nights on the town. One reason I developed such a close bond with my grandmother was the amount of time I spent with her. My mother left me in her care often so that she could go out with her girlfriends.

The alcoholism and refusal to embrace adult responsibilities ultimately ended my mother's relationship with the man that became my stepfather. He was a hard-working truck driver that had managed his money well and we were very comfortable…until my mother began burning through vast amounts of money throwing parties for her friends. At one point she asked for money to build a playhouse for me which my grandmother helped to fund on her fixed income. The "playhouse" was actually an expansive one-room cabin with a bar and dance floor that was constructed right next to our home. I rarely went in the building and can't remember keeping any significant playthings there. She hosted lavish parties in it that were attended by friends that came from a hundred miles away to partake of free booze on my stepfather's dime.

Needless to say, this man who worked hard and paid his bills and lived an otherwise honorable life got tired of my mother's shenanigans and the marriage came to an end. She claimed it was her decision to leave, of course; many alcoholics can never accept a reality where they are at fault for anything. It is far more likely that my stepfather ended it. What I remember about our last day on the farm is that my mother took great pleasure in uprooting some expensive fruit trees that had been planted on either side of the long driveway as we departed. She did not take the trees to replant them at our new residence, just left them there in the dirt. It was a spiteful act that speaks volumes about her alcohol-fueled personality.

A myth that my mother perpetrated over most of her life was that she was inherently "good" or noble because she kept a job and paid her bills.

On the few times I confronted her about her alcoholism she would always counter with "I take care of my job and pay my bills." The truth is that she became a functional alcoholic and did not avoid an occasional reprimand from her employers or even a fender-bender. On one occasion I had to remove her from the premises of a bingo hall that hired her to clean the facility each night. They paid her a salary and supplied her with a small apartment above the bingo hall. She had failed to show up for work on more than one occasion because she was passed out in the apartment. These occasional missteps were never a part of the false narrative she had constructed about her own life.

I think it is very easy for people to delude themselves about the life they're creating. Some people equate the absence of crisis with success. They bob along in the stream of humanity and celebrate getting by without getting *better*. The crises invariably come, however, and it is only in those moments that true character is exposed.

By the time my mother turned 60 her health was in serious decline. She still drank heavily (although not as often) and smoked close to two packs of cigarettes each day. A diagnosis of emphysema did little to curb her destructive lifestyle. She somehow managed to keep her job as a door greeter for Wal-Mart but would often cough and wheeze while standing there providing buggies or checking receipts. I had to pick her up once when she was too ill to finish her shift. One look at her compelled me to drive her straight to the hospital while she railed in protest. The ER doctor immediately summoned a pulmonary specialist. The prognosis he offered was grim.

"This is the deal," the young doctor said. "You have emphysema, and these are your choices. You can quit smoking today and we can manage the emphysema with some degree of success, or you can continue smoking and in a short time you probably won't be here."

If she made an effort to quit it was a weak one. My mother had been smoking for 40 years. Like so many other alcoholics she believed she was invincible. I don't know if my mother ever thought about her life's journey coming to an end. I suspect she thought there was plenty of time to put the cigarettes down.

On the day before Thanksgiving in 1998 I went to a local grocery store to pick up items for my family's holiday dinner. When I walked in to the store I was met by a police officer. It was a small town and I knew most of the men on the force. My brother-in-law at the time, Patrick Garrigan, worked for the department. The officer waiting for me in the store was cordial but something about his demeanor was different that day. He told me without offering an explanation that I could proceed with my shopping but could not leave the store. When Patrick arrived at the store I was sent out to meet him in the parking lot. Many thoughts were tumbling through my head but nothing could have prepared me for the news he was about to deliver.

"Your mother passed away today," Patrick said. "I was called to her home this afternoon by some family members who showed up to visit and could not get a response. I'm very sorry."

Just like that my mother was gone.

As an only child the sole responsibility of making my mother's arrangements was mine. Thankfully, she had been well-insured at Wal-Mart and they were incredibly helpful to me during that difficult time despite the fact that we had to conduct our business on Black Friday, the busiest shopping day of the year. I arrived at the store and was treated like royalty. They made everything as easy on me as possible and allowed me to keep the vest she wore at work.

My mother's final paycheck was given to me. When I saw it I was struck by the amount of unused sick time and vacation time she had accumulated. Even though she was very ill my mother had taken few, if any, days off from work. Her vest was decorated with pins she had received for her efforts.

Her funeral service was attended by her siblings, a few friends, and a small group of co-workers. The minister was someone who had never met my mother before. She had no church affiliation. A few days after the service I cleared out her small rented house of the few possessions she owned. She had no bank account and her purse contained about $25.

Even though my mother worked hard and was surely an asset to some of her employers she left not one thing behind that spoke of purpose or of creating value with the 60 years she'd been given. My mother did not live, she survived. When she left this world I don't recall a single person at her wake or funeral service saying, "What a hard worker she was!" The world was not impacted or impressed by her presence one iota.

I know that to some this will sound harsh. We all want to believe only the best about people, especially in our remembrances of them after they are gone. I have no doubt that my mom made her friends happy, occasionally did good things for others, and had plenty of great qualities. It doesn't matter. Her life was no different than that of a hamster on a wheel. Just keep the wheel turning and get through the day while pretending that everything is great and that tomorrow might offer some possibility beyond the wheel.

There is little nobility in working hard if you have no purpose.

2 THE WORKING LIFE

At 35 years old my life was starting to look a lot like my mother's. There was a divorce in the rearview mirror and plenty of wreckage on the road. My days consisted of just ambling through life without a genuine purpose but that seemed like enough. I was living in a rented home and had no money in the bank. The few items of furniture I owned were second-hand and my other possessions were few. Life had devolved into little more than a process of day-to-day survival.

In retrospect it is easy for me to see how things were aligning for an epic fail. Many people I knew then had it all together. They had been to college and embarked on successful careers. They had bank accounts with actual money in them. Some of them had purchased homes and were halfway to paying off a 20-year mortgage. These young people had found a sense of purpose.

There are two important points I need to make here. First, when I speak of purpose I don't necessarily mean a desire to cure cancer or broker peace in the Gaza. There is purpose in wanting to become financially secure so that your family has fewer struggles. There is purpose in building a career that benefits your local community and gives you a sense of fulfillment. There is purpose in being a good parent. These things might not make the front page of the local paper but they are possessed of a genuine nobility that will motivate you to pursue excellence.

My second point is that not all young people are irresponsible. We read about the ones who are. Not nearly enough attention is given by the mainstream media to those young people who are focused and directed on noble goals. We need to do a better job as a society of celebrating young people that are making good choices by going to college and working hard to contribute to the betterment of our world. One of my greatest regrets is that I did not do a better job harnessing the power of my youth. So much time was wasted that could have been devoted to my own dreams and aspirations.

Thankfully, I did not inherit my mother's alcoholism although I think it could've happened without much encouragement. I've never felt the need to abstain from alcohol and have been intoxicated on more than one occasion (including one memorable instance when I petted a ceramic cat at a Christmas party) but the truth is that I rarely drink. Maybe the reason I don't drink very often is that I'm a little scared of the genetics and what might be lurking inside. My mom wasn't a very nice person when she was drunk. In that regard, at least, I wasn't repeating her mistakes as I hit what is the midway point of life for many people.

The biggest source of pride for me in 2005 was my job. I worked for a transportation company. That's a nice way of saying I drove a taxi for a living. In addition to picking up fares and taking them to the airport or other destinations I also functioned as a courier. Drivers for the taxi company delivered blood from the local blood bank to hospitals across Texas and more than once I was tasked with driving donated organs to a tissue bank in Austin. The company provided Tipsy Taxi service for local events and also operated a limousine. The first time I was asked to drive the limo was on New Year's Eve. It was a little scary and intimidating. After just a few minutes behind the wheel, however, I called the company dispatcher.

"I've got to get one of these!" I said.

There were also two MediCabs in the fleet and I was "qualified" to drive them by virtue of a ten minute training session on how to use the wheelchair lift and secure passengers for transport to and from doctor's offices and nursing homes. On my very first MediCab assignment I made a horrible error when I failed to secure a wheelchair properly and dumped an elderly passenger on the floor as I climbed a small hill leaving the hospital. I was terrified and thought that I had hurt him. Thank goodness he was okay aside from being a little shaken up. On one occasion I arrived at the hospital to pick up an elderly lady who was restrained in her wheelchair. She suffered from dementia and I was called to take her back to her nursing home some thirty miles away. Halfway there she began to have a bad episode in the back of the MediCab. We made it to the care facility but it took several people to calm her down and remove her from the van. Driving the MediCab was my least favorite duty.

On the other hand, driving the taxi was almost always fun and something I enjoyed. People share the most amazing stories from the back seat of a taxicab. I gave rides to rich people, poor people, black people, white people, drug dealers and preachers. Most of them had a unique story to share. I also learned that there were two groups of people who would never try to stiff me on a fare and always tipped better than others: illegal immigrants and prostitutes. The reason was pretty simple. Neither of them wanted trouble. They simply couldn't afford it.

There were some harrowing moments. I drove the night shift from 6 p.m. to 6 a.m. and dealt with my share of people up to no good in the dead of night. When I first started the job my dispatcher had told me something that stuck with me throughout my time as a driver.

"One of these nights," he said, "someone will get into the taxi and the hairs on the back of your neck will stand up. Be ready."

It took a couple of years but it finally happened. Once I was sent to a bad neighborhood at 3 a.m. to pick up a young man from a house that had a reputation as a drug den. Our city charter required us to respond to every call but a driver could refuse the fare if something didn't feel right. Against my better judgment I picked the young man up and he took a seat in the back of the cab directly behind me. This was not something I should have permitted. He told me where he wanted to go and I started the meter. Within minutes I started to feel uneasy. I took the cab's radio in my hand and made sure he could see me holding it, ready to alert dispatch if there was a problem. We made it to the destination and the young man paid his fare without complaint or incident. I began to think I had overreacted to the possibility of trouble.

The next morning I was cleaning my taxi at the end of my shift when I discovered a knife that had been shoved down into the small space where the top and bottom of the back seat met. It was right where the young man had been sitting. To this day I think he had every intention of doing me harm but lost his nerve. Maybe it was me taking up the radio or maybe he just chose not to. Whatever the reason, I am grateful that I escaped without injury. In my whole time as a driver I never once came to physical harm.

I was robbed once and the experience taught me a powerful lesson about profiling people based on their race. From the moment I started working at the taxi company it was instilled in me by dispatchers and the other drivers to take extra care when picking up fares in black neighborhoods. Now, this would be an appropriate time to make a few remarks about my hometown of Tyler, Texas. Tyler has long been saturated with racial tension. Growing up I was aware of it but hate was never something overtly encouraged by my mother or grandmother. Nevertheless, there was always a covert form of racism lurking in the shadows of my family home. I imagine it is the same for almost everyone that grew up in the south. You encountered it often whether or not it was something your family practiced in the open.

When I was robbed it happened on the south side of Tyler, the principal domain of affluent white families. I was sent to an Applebee's to pick up a 30-something white male. I had developed a bad habit of keeping too much money in my change bag and that night I was carrying close to

$700. I had also placed the change bag on the floorboard by my feet. I didn't know it but the bag had slid beneath the seat right into the rear of the cab. I did not realize it had been taken until the same person that took it paid me with my own money and even gave me a healthy tip.

I am grateful that, especially as I have gotten older, I am able to separate character from a person's race. It is something I also tried to instill in my daughter. When Hurricane Rita hit Texas and Louisiana in 2005 my daughter and I were spending a few nights in a shelter that had been set up at the CenturyLink Center in Bossier City. On our second day there I awoke from a nap and was unable to find my daughter. In a panic I began to search the large arena asking everyone in sight if they had seen my child. An elderly black lady approached me and told me that my daughter was volunteering to help new arrivals procure cots and blankets. The lady was lost and reeling after the double whammy of storms that had hit the region, first Katrina which devastated New Orleans and then Rita which slammed Texas. She told me that my daughter had approached her when she arrived at the shelter and showed her where to get food and other necessities. A short time later I found my daughter still working to assist the steady flow of new arrivals.

I've made plenty of mistakes in my life, without question, but in that moment I knew I had done something right in instilling important values in my child.

In reality most of my time as a taxi driver and courier were great. I worked with some good people. One of them was a cheerful guy that was a dead ringer for Robert Shaw as Quint from *Jaws*. We often worked the weekends together and would hang out at a local convenience store between calls. I was tasked once with picking up former vice president Dan Quayle. I was tempted to challenge him to an impromptu spelling bee. Chubby Checker and Jermaine Jackson were passengers in the company taxis. Most of all I enjoyed many of the regular people I picked up, those men and women who depended on the taxi service to go to work or the grocery store.

On the Thanksgiving holiday the company always ran a skeleton crew and served a meal for its employees at the cabstand. There was a family-like atmosphere at the company and I was enjoying myself. I was a bachelor and could come and go as I pleased, slept during the day and stayed up all night. Life was about as good as it gets for someone without a purpose that compels them to be more than they are.

After more than a year as a driver I was approached by one of the owners of the company and offered a promotion to dispatcher. It seemed like a great deal. I would have regular, mid-shift hours—2 p.m. until 10 p.m.—and be guaranteed a certain income each week. As a driver my income varied according to the season and current gas prices. I was also given the freedom to drive a shift now and again on my days off or in the mornings if I wanted to make some extra money. With little thought or consideration I accepted the offer and began a new phase of my transportation career.

Things worked out great. I used the extra time off to start writing again, mostly original songs. I moved into a better apartment close to the hospital district on the east side of the same street where I had grown up. It was a garage apartment—I'm guessing they were built during the 1960's—that was quaint and cool. The taxi company also allowed me to take my cab home each day so I had wheels without the maintenance or upkeep that comes with owning a car.

Then, without any warning whatsoever, my life was turned upside down.

3 SINGLE DAD

The phone rang one day while I was sitting in the dispatch chair and I paid it no attention. This was standard. It was, after all, a taxi company. Someone was calling 24/7.

"Scotty, you have a call on line one," the receptionist announced from a room adjoining the dispatch office.

I picked up the phone. "Hello?"

It was my ex-wife, Becky, calling from Minnesota. We divorced after a lengthy marriage and it was as much my fault as hers, maybe even more. We married young after dating for just one month. Throughout our marriage I shuffled between numerous jobs and we moved multiple times. It wasn't an ideal life for either of us but we tried for ten years to make it work. The one bright spot we shared was our daughter, Paige. Since Becky never called me at work and rarely called me at all I must have instinctively known that the call was about our child.

The icy fingers of dread began to massage my spine. I think most parents have been in the "phone call" situation or accept that they might be sooner or later. Whenever our kids are away from the nest we pray that no one calls with bad news. As I listened to what my ex-wife had to say my heart sank down in the depths of sadness. There had been an incident of abuse in the home involving my daughter. It was deemed in my Paige's best interest that she come to live with me and that I be given temporary full custody.

It is very hard to describe all of the emotions I experienced during that phone call. My initial sadness flowed into worry for Paige and then anger at the person capable of doing this to her. There was some sense of joy that she would be coming back to Texas and living with me but at that moment I just wanted to reach through the telephone lines and hug her.

From the day Paige was born we were thick as thieves. I changed her diapers, fed her at all hours of the day and night, and bonded with her at every opportunity. She was a daddy's girl from the very beginning and seeing her move so far away was heartbreaking. The move made visits every other weekend impossible. I was able to see Paige once a year in the summer for four to six weeks. When I first began to see her for the summer I did not even own a car. The taxi company had to send someone to pick me up for work each day. On two occasions I had to take a Greyhound bus from Texas to Minnesota to pick her up and take her back. It was a 21-hour trip one way and the same bus that arrived in her town was the one departing to come back to Texas. The round trip demanded I spend 42 hours straight on a Greyhound bus. It didn't matter; I would have ridden for a month just to see Paige for a day.

Within minutes of hanging up the phone I was making arrangements. I immediately marched into the office of the owner of the company and informed him of what was going on. I was still living paycheck-to-paycheck and did not have the money for a plane ticket. He began clicking keys on his computer and quickly booked an airline ticket for my daughter. I had no way to pay for it but my boss told me we would worry about that later.

"Just get your daughter," he said.

The company really stepped up for me in that situation and I am still grateful. What I didn't realize at that moment was how dependent I'd become upon my job and how that dependency was going to impact the next ten years of my life. I was confusing that dependency with a false sense of security, and security is something that needs to exist beyond the perimeter of a job. I'd built no safety net whatsoever to protect me in the event of losing my income.

The next morning a friend of mine and fellow driver at the company drove me to DFW International Airport. When Paige stepped off the plane I was overcome with emotion. She was thin and her once-beautiful long hair was matted and unkempt but she was happy to see her dad. We drove home and set about the business of designing our new life together.

My life had taken another turn that made it resemble my mother's. So many questions went through my mind. Was I equipped to raise a child by myself, especially a daughter approaching her teenage years? Would I repeat the mistakes of my own mother and fail in my parental obligations? I'm not sure if it was a subconscious refusal to address these questions but I think I regressed into that attitude of false nobility I mentioned at the beginning of this book. Just work and keep food on the table and the lights on, Scotty, and everything else will be okay.

And it was…until it wasn't.

Paige went to school and I went to work. She thrived under my care and we renewed that bond between us. We were close again. On some evenings we would go out to eat or walk across the street for a pizza and bring it home. On others I would cook one of her favorite meals. We huddled around the television during football season and cheered for the Pittsburgh Steelers—Paige's favorite team and mine, too, when I was her age. We went to movies when we could and geeked out together when we witnessed Anakin Skywalker's transformation into Darth Vader. It was a blissful period for both of us.

Early on it was obvious that my small garage apartment wasn't going to be adequate. It was small and I wanted to be sure Paige felt like she had a measure of privacy, her own space. I began looking for a new place to live as soon as she arrived but finding something I could afford was difficult. One day my boss at the taxi company told me he had a nice two-bedroom rental available. It was a little more than what I wanted to spend each month but it was large and the bedrooms were on opposite ends of the house. I agreed to rent the place after a hasty walk-through and we moved in right away.

It became apparent that we were not the only ones calling the place home. The house was infested with cockroaches. Bold, in-your-face cockroaches. If there had been any way to back out of the rental agreement at that moment I think I would have done it, but there was no way to get my old apartment back. We were stuck.

Herein is a great life lesson. Are you listening?

What do you do when your house is teeming with cockroaches?

You get rid of the cockroaches.

I did everything necessary to remove every cockroach from our new home in a very short period of time. Within days they were gone. I put out boric acid along the floorboards. I made sure all the food was secured and kept no garbage in the house. In short, I made our house an inhospitable domain for cockroaches. Whether they died from the boric acid or packed their bags and moved was not my concern. I only know that they were gone.

Whatever environment you want to create in your life is possible if you want it bad enough and are willing to do whatever it takes to make it a reality. If you settle for substandard, substandard is what you will get.

4 SAILING WITHOUT A COMPASS

2005 came and brought with it several things. The beginning of another year on the job. The beginning of another year with my precious daughter who was doing well in school and learning how to trust again. The beginning of another year of paying the bills and getting by and living from day-to-day with no sense of purpose or direction.

With my tax refund in 2005 I was able to purchase a used car. It was a Ford Taurus and got great gas mileage. Paige and I now had the freedom to go more places than we were permitted to go in the taxi I'd been bringing home for over a year, and let's face facts. No respectable 13 year-old girl wants to be picked up at school by a taxi even if her dad is behind the wheel. *Especially* if her dad is behind the wheel. I even allowed her to choose which car I was going to buy when we went to the lot. She picked a good one. We brought it home, slapped a Bruce Springsteen bumper sticker on it, and took a maiden voyage to Six Flags over Texas in Arlington to celebrate. I'd used a small portion of the tax refund to buy each of us a season pass. As I was recalling this memory the words of Springsteen's "Used Cars" came to mind:

> *"Now mister the day my number comes in,*
> *I ain't ever gonna ride in no used car again."*

It would be incorrect to say that I didn't have visions and dreams of a better life. I did. I think wanting more is common to most people and I think it's healthy. There is nothing wrong with wanting to better yourself. The problem is not with the desire to elevate ourselves but with our unwillingness to make the conscious endeavor required to do just that. For many people dreams are just dreams because there is no purpose to give them fuel. That's the boat I was blissfully sailing across the expanse of time in 2005, unmindful of the inevitability of reaching a final destination or of the jagged rocks lurking beneath the surface. A man with no purpose is like a ship with no captain at the wheel. The boat will eventually land somewhere even if that somewhere is at the bottom of the ocean in a thousand pieces. Refusing to make a choice to improve yourself is making a choice to be dashed on the rocks.

Most of my dreams centered on a writing career. Since my youth I had shown a desire to write and a genuine talent for it. When I was about seven years old I would watch news reports on television and then write my own version of events. I'd put on the nicest clothes I owned and take my "copy" to the bathroom where I would read it standing before the mirror, my pretend television monitor. By the time I entered the fifth grade those rewritten news stories were appearing in a school paper that was started by one of the teachers to encourage students to write creatively.

In high school I discovered Stephen King and began a love affair with his work that continues to this very day. In my earliest attempts to write serious fiction I tried to emulate the master. All I wanted to write was horror stories. King had nothing to fear from those initial efforts. The truth is that I spent a lot of time dreaming about being a successful writer and almost none working to improve my craft.

Dreams and goals are great. Wanting to lose weight and stay healthy is a great goal. I heard someone say once that they didn't exercise but read about it instead to stay motivated to start. They were up to 100 pages a day! Staying motivated is only a part of the equation. If you aren't staying active in the pursuit of the life you envision it doesn't matter how motivated you are. A key step in making a conscious endeavor is to *move*. You must be an active participant in your own success. If you aren't you'll be a passive participant in your own failure.

In November of 1991 I was given a gift of such magnitude that the day on which I received it is forever red-lettered in my memory. My ex-wife and I were living in Nacogdoches, Texas where I was working as a manager trainee for Popeye's Chicken. One night I looked across the counter and saw author Joe R. Lansdale on the other side. Joe has written numerous novels, short stories, and films including Bubba Ho-Tep, Cold in July, and the Hap and Leonard books which are currently being turned into a series for the Sundance television channel. Joe was standing there in a crew jacket from one of the Texas Chainsaw Massacre films and I was in fanboy heaven.

While Joe waited on his takeout order I spoke to him about being a fan of his work and my own writing aspirations. I'm quite sure Joe had heard similar talk many times before but he was courteous and listened.

What happened next was incredible.

"Why don't you give me a call in a few days and I'll try to put some stuff together for you that might help. Suggest some markets to try."

You can probably imagine how excited I was. I wanted to call him right away but somehow restrained myself and waited for about a week. When he answered the phone I couldn't believe I was talking to one of my idols. Joe gave me the address of his home in Nacogdoches and a time to meet.

The day of our meeting was cold, gray, and damp, perfect for a horror fan meeting a famous writer of scary stories. Joe opened the door, phone in hand, and motioned for me to take a seat in his living room while he finished his call. I won't even pretend that I wasn't trying to listen to Joe's end. From what I could gather he was discussing an upcoming Batman project. *That* Batman. The Caped Crusader. Na-na-na-na, Na-na-na-na…Batman!

I thought I was going to faint.

Joe finished his call and said, "Let's go down to my office."

I remember walking into this large room with a modest desk and cabinets on the wall. There was martial arts gear in the room and a round table that was covered with copies of small press horror magazines. Beautiful long windows offered a view of the woods around Joe's house. I also remember thinking how this was the kind of workspace I needed to get inspired. Surely that was one of my problems. I was living with my pregnant wife and stepson in a two bedroom trailer that barely offered enough room to move. The kitchen was so small I considered getting a stool that would rotate so I could just spin around while making dinner instead of getting up and bumping into the appliances. Yes, this explained my lack of success. I had not yet found the ideal space to create.

Joe asked me about my writing efforts and I went into the standard spiel about how hard I was working and how certain I was that success was just around the corner. To his credit Joe did not so much as wrinkle his nose at the odorous pile of bullshit that was now contaminating his working environment. Looking back on it I am grateful that the writing gods did not strike me down for blasphemy on the spot.

Then came the anticipated moment of my pilgrimage to the Nacogdoches woods. I steeled myself as the lightning flashed and the thunder rumbled and the angelic voices of a heavenly artistic choir swelled inside my head. With all due reverence I posed the question I had come to ask.

"What is the secret of being a successful writer?"

The room got very quiet. I felt like Moses on the mountain. In just a moment fire would burst forth and deliver the divine wisdom, leaving a holy glow on my face. Joe regarded me with a serious look. My stomach made a *bluh-bluh-blup* noise as I stood there in nervous awe.

Wait for it.

"Put ass to chair in front of typewriter," Joe said. He then turned around and walked over to the table covered with magazines and began to pick through the pile. That was it. I stood there for a moment, sure that more was coming. Joe gave me an armful of magazines, took several of his own books from the cabinets on the wall, and ushered me back to the main part of the house. We sat at his dining table while he autographed each book for me.

While he signed the books Joe told me about his early days as a writer. He spoke about working long hours at a regular job and coming home late at night. He said there was a late movie on one of the local television stations and that he would watch that while he wound down from work. When the movie was over he would retreat to a small, cramped space and write for hours. Finally, he would grab some sleep…not nearly enough I am guessing…and the next day start the whole process over again. That was his routine and he did it every day. No exceptions. As he told me about this Joe often stared into the space between us as though he were reliving every moment. It was very apparent that the sacrifices he made to realize his dream were not lost on him.

It took almost twenty years for me to realize that I had been given a great gift that day. Joe's advice went so far beyond the art of writing. There was a deeper meaning in his words that is applicable to success in any endeavor. People who achieve their goals are not passive observers of life. They are active creators of the reality they desire. No price is too great, no effort is too great, and no sacrifice is too great for the person that will not be denied their dream.

My response to Joe's advice at the time he gave it was to return home with my autographed books and dreams where I fell right back into the grind of living. Survival. There was no great sense of urgency. *I'm only 25 years old*, I thought at the time.

Now, here I was on the south side of 35 and the only writing I had published was a few sports articles for a small weekly paper. Every so often I would open up my computer and try to write something…anything…but the effort never lasted more than a few days at a time.

The man who dares to sail through life without a compass is at the mercy of his environment. Sooner or later the winds will change and angry storm clouds will begin to materialize on the horizon.

5 SHIPWRECK

When I was a freshman in high school our band took a trip to Daytona Beach to compete in an invitational concert event. The competition was a formality, though, and little more than a way to justify the trip to the school board. The band took one of these trips every four years and it was exciting. My good fortune of taking the trip as a freshman meant taking a second one again as a senior. It would be my first time to visit Florida and the itinerary included spending a day at Walt Disney World in Orlando. I was especially looking forward to this because the EPCOT Center had just opened. I was a geek then and remain a geek today.

There was, of course, plenty of time to frolic in the waters of the Atlantic Ocean in between band competitions and trips to the amusement park. One day I was out in the water swimming and enjoying myself and not paying very much attention to my surroundings. I looked up and discovered that I was pretty far away from the beach. The closest person to me was a senior classmate, Mitchell Stevenson, about fifteen feet away. With a growing sense of panic I noticed that my feet weren't touching the ocean floor and that each wave seemed to take me out even farther. I began to yell for help. Mitchell saw my struggles and began swimming in my direction. Somehow he was able to reach me and pull me out of what was probably a riptide. I was from Texas and didn't know much about those things back then, but a few years later I observed from the beach in Galveston as a friend of mine and his son were swept out quickly. They managed to stay together and escape but the experience was harrowing.

By the way…if you happen to be reading this, Mitchell Stevenson, thanks. The events in this book that came after that trip might not have happened without you.

You know, life can be a lot like a riptide. We can get so caught up in bobbing up and down with the waves that we lose perspective and fail to realize we're in deep water. That's how the seduction of time works when we live without a sense of purpose. The days just march by and pretty soon we look back and see that we're 30 or 35 years out to sea. When I realized the riptide of life had me in its clutches there was no one there to pull me back in. I had two choices. Swim or drown.

For a few months I had been dating one of my co-workers at the taxi company. Ever since my divorce five years earlier I had not dated and it was nice to have a relationship again, although in retrospect I would probably advise against relationships in the workplace. Paige had a little difficulty adjusting to it as well and not long after she came to live with me the relationship cooled. I think my new girlfriend and I both understood that my priorities had changed. Sharing me just wasn't something my daughter was willing to do at that point, and who can blame her? The young lady and I continued to work together and remained friends even though we no longer had a romantic involvement.

During this same period of time the taxi company had undergone a management change. The previous owners of the company, two brothers from Iran, had returned as partners. The older of the two brothers was a smart, professional businessman. He was tough but fair in his dealings with employees and I respected him. The younger of the two, whom I will call Haji, was the complete opposite. He was unprofessional and often engaged in questionable behavior on the job. There was some speculation that he was engaged in an affair with a daughter of an employee. I didn't get wrapped up in the office drama Haji always seemed to be at the center of. I just stayed clear of him as much as possible.

When my relationship ended Haji took pleasure in taunting me about it, often while I was driving. He would make remarks on the dispatch radio which could be heard by every driver and passenger in the company taxis. It made me uncomfortable and I took my concerns to management. The majority owner, a man named Archer, was sympathetic but took no identifiable action to prevent another occurrence.

The taunting continued until one day I simply could not take it anymore. The jibes were becoming infused with sexual innuendo. I drove to a nearby convenience store, parked the taxi, and called the office. I was so distressed that I was shaking and on the verge of tears, a good sign that my unhappiness was rapidly turning to anger. Archer told me to come to the cabstand.

When I arrived Archer ushered me into his office where Haji was waiting. I voiced my concerns and told the Haji his behavior was offensive and inappropriate. He was angered that I would dare to make a complaint and laughed at me before becoming very serious.

"I think you need to quit," he said.

Quit! I couldn't believe this was happening. "No, I will not quit."

"Yes, you quit."

Despite my protests I was told to go home by Archer and take a day off. I wasn't eager to leave with the status of my job in doubt. The whole scene was surreal. I had total faith in the company. In all my years there I'd never had a reason to question the integrity of management. I truly believed that I was doing the right thing by voicing my complaint and that the company would do the right thing in return. I didn't want Haji to get in trouble. I just wanted him to stop. No harm, no foul.

To my horror Archer would not verbally acknowledge I was being fired but made it clear that my employment with the company was over. This was the man that had helped me secure a plane ticket for my daughter! I left the cabstand in shock. No scenario I had envisioned included the possibility of losing my job.

It was late morning when I returned home. Paige was in school and would not be home for several hours. I sat in my house and wondered how I was going to explain this to her. What would her reaction be? She'd been through so much and the last thing she needed was to incur further stress on my account. I took time to gather myself and did what many people do in times of crisis. I talked myself into believing that everything was going to work out okay. By the time I picked Paige up from school I had calmed myself and began to formulate a plan. We talked about what had happened and I assured her that we were going to be okay.

Later that night in the privacy of my bedroom I stayed awake for hours. I had less than a few hundred dollars to my name. The rent, utilities, and car payment would all be due soon. I knew that the vessel I'd been sailing had wrecked and was taking on water.

If I didn't find a way to right the ship, and soon, my daughter and I were going to sink.

6 HOMELESS

This is how I became homeless in America: I made poor choices.

My belief is that a person's life is dictated largely by the choices they make. When I first conceived the idea of telling my story in a book it was very important to me that my account be honest and that it involve taking personal responsibility for many of my hardships.

I want to tread carefully here because I don't want anyone that is struggling to think I am unsympathetic to their plight, but I also feel strongly about the importance of owning one's circumstances no matter what they may be. In looking back over my life I realize that taking that scholarship in high school would have been a better choice. Getting an education and using that education to build a career would have been a better choice. Working harder to hone my skills as a writer and putting my "ass to chair in front of typewriter" as Joe Lansdale suggested would have been a better choice. Something I have learned through my own struggles is that a victim mentality does not empower, it does not serve. It only erodes and imprisons the human spirit.

After losing my job at the taxi company there was a glimmer of hope in the realization that when the company promoted me to dispatcher they also made me a salaried employee instead of an independent contractor. Drivers were pretty much on their own if they were terminated but dispatchers were paid a weekly salary and therefore potentially eligible for unemployment benefits if they were released. I went right away to the Texas Employment Commission and filed for benefits to sustain my daughter and myself while I looked for work. The benefits weren't expected to be much; my salary was only $350 per week. Whatever they gave me would help until I could find work again.

The taxi company would attempt to dispute my claim. I knew this without a doubt. They had a lot to lose. My version of events might cause them to be investigated or fined for their behavior. The only way for the company to avoid the possibility of a negative backlash would be to discredit me and attempt to cover up their actions. Anyone bold enough to tell me I quit when I did no such thing would have no problem lying to the TEC. It was my word against the word of the company. The two owners present on the day of my firing would corroborate one another's testimony. Sure enough, I received a letter from the TEC stating that my claim had been contested.

There was an ace up my sleeve that they didn't know about—my former girlfriend. She was still driving for the company but agreed to offer testimony on my behalf that would support my claim that Haji had been making inappropriate comments on the two-way radios that were used in every cab. We met to discuss her testimony and she even gave me a handwritten statement that we would also submit into evidence.

While I waited for the TEC to set a hearing date my first benefit check arrived. It came just in time, too. The utilities were past due and our food supply was dwindling. On one night we had to split a can of beans for dinner. Once the bills were caught up I bought a little food and stuck back the rest of the money. The benefit checks only came once every two weeks. I had to make it last.

A telephone hearing was scheduled. I was informed that a claims investigator from the TEC would hear testimony from myself, my witness, and the owners of the company. Her decision in the matter would be final. I had to join the hearing from the TEC office in Tyler while my former employers were allowed to participate from their place of business. I arrived early and hoped my former girlfriend would do the same so that we could go over her testimony one last time. As the appointed hour drew near a sense of dread settled in the pit of my stomach and grew by the minute. My former girlfriend had not shown up. I tried calling her but there was no answer. I tried to buy some extra time but the hearing began without her. My suspicion was that the company had somehow learned of her intention to testify and "discouraged" her somehow. Perhaps they sent her on a courier run at the scheduled time or perhaps they simply paid her not to show up. It is even possible that she just decided not to get involved. She was working to support three children of her own so I couldn't really blame her in any case.

Over the course of the next hour the owners of the company presented a dishonest version of events in an effort to protect themselves. Not only did they claim I quit but they also made efforts to discredit me. I gave my side of the story without a single person to validate it. The TEC ruled that I should not receive further unemployment assistance and that I would have to repay the benefits I had already received.

The TEC's decision was devastating. Somehow I was going to have to find a way to repay money that had already been used for bills and food. My initial attempts to find work had been unsuccessful. The majority of my work experience consisted of food service jobs and my time at the taxi company. I had successfully pigeon-holed myself as a common laborer, and common labor jobs were in short supply.

Now, I've heard it said by many people that if someone really wants to work they can find a job. I'm not going to dispute this. Could I have taken a minimum wage job at a burger joint? Probably. Any reasonable person should be able to see the folly in this. The money I earned wouldn't have come close to what we needed to survive. What about a second job? Perhaps. It's possible that doing that could have wound up *costing* me more than what the job paid because it would have necessitated some form of childcare for Paige. At the very least someone would have to pick her up from school each day. Paige was thirteen but after everything she had been through there was no way I was going to leave her alone for hours. The next time you encounter someone that is unemployed try not to be too judgmental and realize that the inability to find a job does not automatically equal an unwillingness to work.

Driving home from that meeting was misery. What were my daughter and I going to do? We had just enough money to make it through a couple of months.

As bad as being denied unemployment insurance was I had no idea just how bad things were about to get. You might recall that the house I had rented earlier in the year…the one that was teeming with cockroaches when we moved in…was owned by the majority owner of the taxi company. It didn't take Archer long to inform me that I would need to make new living arrangements. When we moved in I had not signed a lease. Archer didn't offer one. It was a month-to-month arrangement and could be terminated at any time. It didn't matter that we had been good tenants and paid rent.

I managed to find a two-bedroom apartment on short notice. The rent was much higher than what we had been paying. It took everything I had in reserve to put down the security deposit and first month's rent. We moved in and I used what little money we had left to buy food. I was flat broke and had just one month to find a job that would pay the bills.

I'm not sure my daughter ever grasped just how dire our situation was and that was fine by me. It wasn't her job to worry about how we were going to make it. That was my job and mine alone. I felt like a colossal failure on so many levels but the worst hurt came from feeling like I had failed my daughter as a parent. There are no words to describe watching the days of that month pass by without finding work. To me it felt like awaiting a date with the executioner. I knew what was coming and was powerless to stop it. The hours sped up and before I knew it I was out of time.

One month after moving in Paige and I drove away from the new apartment with what belongings we could load in my Ford Taurus. We were forced to leave many things behind. I insisted on most of them being mine so that I could take more of her things.

We were officially homeless.

7 ON THE ROAD

There was one thing I could be happy about: Paige finished the current school year before we took to living in my Ford Taurus. I could only hope that by the time the next school year began we would be settled.

In the immediate aftermath of losing our home I made an effort to secure temporary shelter provided by the Salvation Army at a large facility in Tyler. When we arrived I was asked a few questions about our situation and then told we could stay for one night. One night of sleep under a roof and on a bed. The next morning we would have to leave the shelter. I met other people there that had been in residence for extended periods, many of them with little hope of ever leaving. I'm not sure they were even making an effort to leave. My perception was that the Salvation Army was a good organization, and I still believe they do many wonderful things, but after being allowed one night in their shelter I was forced to reevaluate my opinions. The people working there were rude at best and one of them was simply hateful. I don't mean for this to reflect an attempt to characterize the Salvation Army as a whole; I know that there are many good people working in that organization. It would be unfair to the Salvation Army to evaluate their merits based on one or two employees or volunteers.

My experience at the shelter was only the beginning of my introduction to how homeless people are treated in America. One of the saddest confessions I must make in this book is that there were times in my life when I was uncaring and dismissive of the homeless. I never went out of my way to hurt them but I passed up many people on the street. I know now that those people needed to eat, that they would have been thankful for just one night under a roof. I know now how their hearts were breaking at the sight of their children sleeping on the sidewalk or a box.

Not too long ago I logged on to Facebook and saw a news article about so-called Homeless Laws in America. These laws make it a crime for homeless people to be in certain areas or to even sit in specific places. Homelessness is not a crime and we must stop punishing those who find themselves in this predicament. Sometimes all a man has left is his good name. The final humiliation is to have that taken along with everything else because he dared to rest in the wrong spot and was taken to jail.

After leaving the shelter we stayed in the general area of Tyler while I tried to find some kind of work. The desperation was growing now and the cycle that homeless people fall into was beginning to emerge. It would take at least a month of steady employment to earn enough money for a deposit and rent. That meant going to work for one month in wrinkled clothes with no place to take a regular shower. It also meant leaving Paige in the car outside for an entire shift; there was no money to pay a sitter and no one was willing to keep her. I had one friend throughout the entire time that offered to let us stay, again for one night. I'm not upset with him. He was also a single dad raising a young son and his place was very small. There were no family members I could turn to. We had the car and each other.

It occurred to me that perhaps the employment opportunities would be better in Louisiana. I might even be able to find work again as a taxi driver in Shreveport with all of the casinos there. With what little money I was able to obtain we headed east on the I-20. Paige was excited. To her it seemed like a vacation trip. Children are amazing creatures. They can somehow find a way to pretend things aren't broken. They do it with their toys and they do it with their life.

When we got to Shreveport I used some of the money to get a cheap hotel room that offered discounted rates on a weekly basis. Unless I was able to begin working soon we wouldn't be able to stay more than a couple of weeks but that first night we stayed there was pure heaven. We were both able to take a hot shower for the first time in many days. There were even two beds instead of one and no bed has ever felt so good. Included in the room rate was a free full breakfast each morning. It became our habit to eat in the mornings like ravenous hyenas. We would sneak some pastries back to our room for later and at night it was Taco Bell. For less than five dollars we could both have a couple of tacos.

I didn't like leaving Paige at the motel while I looked for work. Some of the employees there were very kind and promised to keep an eye on her or help her if she needed anything while I was gone. I wouldn't leave for more than an hour or so at a time but even that short span made me feel irresponsible.

The local taxi service was a bust. I found out right away that there were several of them. As a former driver I knew that this could be a way for me to earn cash immediately. As independent contractors taxi drivers are paid by each fare and then must pay the company a certain amount of money to lease the taxi for a shift. If I could land a job my first fare would put money in my pocket and I would be on the fast track to recovery.

There was no chance for me to drive a taxi in Shreveport. I'm sure that competition for these jobs was fierce because of the casinos. Drivers here made a good living and every taxi driver within a hundred miles probably wanted a piece of the action. It wouldn't have surprised me if there was a waiting list to lease taxis.

It was discouraging to say the least. I had managed to scrape a few more dollars together from friends or selling more personal possessions but soon those avenues would be closed. There were times when I prayed for night to fall because the few hours of sleep I got was the only time I was even close to being at peace. Paige seemed to be okay...on the outside at least. I was soon to discover that she was suffering inside even worse than I was. She woke up one morning and the right side of her face was drooped. I was thrown into a panic and drove us back to Tyler where we visited a local emergency room. My driver's license still showed that I was a Texas resident. They had to assess Paige regardless of my inability to pay.

A doctor examined Paige and made a diagnosis of Bell's Palsy, or idiopathic facial paralysis. It typically affects older men and women and is often exacerbated by stress. The doctor said that he had never seen it in someone so young. He prescribed steroidal medications as well as medicine for pain relief and assured me it would go away in a week or so. It did, but the message was clear: our situation was causing my daughter pain. I've sometimes wondered how often a single heart can break.

Eventually, I stopped counting.

Filling the prescriptions took more of our limited funds but there was never a question in that regard. At that point I was more than ready to beg on the street if necessary. When most of us think about America we don't think of people begging for help. It isn't the first impression our strong nation conjures. I saw many things during my period of homelessness that seemed to contradict the image of America as a land of equal opportunity.

Our room in Louisiana was a safe haven while Paige took her medicine and began to show signs of recovery. I was out driving the I-20 one day when I saw a big sign that was an advertisement for Harrah's Louisiana Downs. The legendary racetrack was familiar to me. I'd never been there but my mother had been many times in the track's heyday during the 1980's. Those were the days when horses like Sunday Silence and Alysheba competed in the track's marquee event, the Super Derby, and drew thousands in attendance. I told Paige about watching famous horses win the Triple Crown on television when I was her age and suggested we take a day off to visit the races. General admission was free. I called to make sure Paige was old enough to attend with a parent and she was. She needed something...anything...to give her a brief respite from the pressure cooker we were living in.

The little trip was an even better medicine than the steroids. Paige became fascinated with the horses and jockeys. After each race she would stand by the rail and congratulate the winning riders as they returned to the jock's room to prepare for another race. One of the most successful jockeys at the track that summer was a Canadian rider named Jeff Burningham. He was fun to watch because he did a great job coming from behind to win races. It was thrilling. Jeff became Paige's favorite rider. She would wait for him after each race and always shout "Good job!" whether he won or lost. Finally, Jeff stopped to talk to her for a few minutes.

She wanted to go again the next day and I was all for it. It cost us nothing to get in and there were free sodas in the casino area of the track. I would sneak down there every once in a while to get some for us. At the end of the races that day we were getting ready to leave when Jeff Burningham and his wife Lacie passed us in the lower grandstand as they got ready to go home. To my surprise Jeff struck up a conversation and introduced us to his wife. We talked for a while and Jeff talked us into coming back on Wednesday of the following week.

When we got back to the hotel I started to think about a few things. Surely there had to be people taking care of all those horses. Who fed them? Who cleaned their stalls? I began to think that maybe there was an opportunity here for work. The great thing was that I now had an inside contact that might be able to help me secure a job. I hoped I could find something. There was not enough money to rent the room again and our time there was up very soon.

Wednesday rolled around and we went to the track again. Paige cheered for Jeff and met some of the other jockeys as well. It was very surprising to me after the races when Jeff offered to take us out to dinner. My daughter could hardly contain her excitement. On the way to the restaurant we reminded each other how important it was to eat like civilized people. We were so hungry that I was afraid we would order too much and gobble it down in haste.

The meal was the nicest we'd had in almost two months. Jeff and Lacie were such sweet people. We talked about racing and Jeff's own background. I almost choked on my dinner when he told me that he had lived in a small feed room on the track when he was starting out. It was clear that he had also suffered hardships. I wanted to tell him about mine but my pride held my tongue fast. As we were getting ready to leave the restaurant Jeff asked me what I did for a living.

"I work for a transportation company," I blurted.

What was I doing? Here was someone that might be able to help me find work on the track. All I had to do was swallow my pride and be honest. Why I couldn't do it is something I still don't understand.

"You have a very kind daughter," Jeff said, and there was something about the look in his eyes right then that told me he knew. He knew I had no job and no home. I believe that complimenting my daughter was Jeff's way of trying to get through to me. He was saying, *Let us help*. He probably knew that appealing to me by invoking the sweetness of my little girl would touch something in me and make me come clean. Jeff was trying to help me in a way that allowed me to preserve my dignity and I stood there stiff-necked and stubborn.

My daughter didn't say anything when we got back to the motel but I knew she also understood that Jeff was reaching out.

She never once displayed the disappointment that I knew was in her heart.

8 STORMS BEFORE THE STORM

A person cannot assume the task of writing a memoir without recalling some painful experiences. I knew when I started writing mine that this chapter would be difficult but necessary.

My pride had prevented me from telling Jeff Burningham the truth about my situation. I began to pay for it the next week. There was not enough money in my pocket to continue renting the motel room. We were back in the car.

That summer was especially hot in Louisiana. In the daytime I was able to offer Paige some respite from the heat by taking her to the racetrack to watch Jeff ride or by killing a few hours in a store. When night fell, however, there was little I could do to provide even the most rudimentary comforts.

The Ford Taurus was small. Paige would recline in the front passenger seat to sleep while I cramped my body in the back. Sometimes we would switch and I would take the front. It was not uncommon for the temperature to still be close to 100 degrees at nine or ten in the evening. I'm very hot natured to begin with and the heat made resting impossible, not that I could have slept much anyway. I would often look over at Paige, her little body bent into an awkward shape in the seat, and experience a sadness so palpable that it could cause actual, physical pain. It was always a silent pain which, to my mind, is the worst kind. The last thing I wanted was for her to wake up and see the anguish on my face.

There are times even now that I wake up from a dream about those days and nights in the car. There are feelings of panic, of intense fear, but these soon give way to an immeasurable sadness. It is like experiencing it all again as a mere observer who is powerless to change the tragedy playing out before their eyes.

My insomnia on those sultry nights prompted me to rummage through a handful of books that I'd managed to keep. Most of my book collection had been sold along with DVDs and other media. There may have been ten books in total left. After Paige fell asleep I would read from one until the night cooled or I simply became too exhausted to stay awake. Books have always been a source of escape for me and I guess that is what I was trying to do through those pages.

Henry David Thoreau's book *Walden* had always held some interest for me. Rediscovering it, however, planted the seed of something that would ultimately impact my ability to recover. I didn't know it then, of course. I think at that particular moment in my life I was searching and maybe the answers could have been provided by any book. It would be far more romantic for me to say that Thoreau somehow called to me and made me choose his work from others, but I think the truth is that Thoreau's words were the words I was willing to hear at the time. They were the words that resonated with me and were able to pierce through my cynicism and bitterness to touch a part of me that was dimming by the day.

I was gripped by Thoreau's premise. Dissatisfied with his own life and the life he saw others creating, Thoreau essentially decided to become what we would call homeless and move to the Maine woods...on *purpose*. It was hard for me to understand why anyone would forego the comforts of a real home in exchange for a cabin in the woods with the bugs, snakes, and snow. Thoreau claimed that he wanted to simplify his life and distill it down to the most basic elements, but what was he trying to prove? The answer began to make itself clear when I encountered the following passage:

"I am convinced of no greater fact than the unquestionable ability of man to elevate his life by a conscious endeavor."

Thoreau seemed to believe that he had control of his own destiny, an inherent power to raise himself to great heights. I still wasn't sold on how moving to the woods was going to accomplish that but for the first time there was a spark of hope that struggled to illuminate my inner and outer darkness. It was weak but it was there. Thoreau and I established a type of communion that was as powerful to me as the Eucharist.

The days, weeks, and months passed by. Our meals consisted of a single taco once a day unless we were invited to dinner by Jeff and Lacie. They did that at least once a week. I'm sure it was Jeff's way of helping us in a way that did not violate his refusal to press the issue of offering aid. Sometimes we would sneak into our old motel at night and quietly make our way to the swimming pool. Being careful not to make noise we would bathe in the pool with pieces of soap I'd saved. The nighttime routine was always the same—find a safe place to park the car and sleep. Sometimes I had to drive many miles to find a rest area where I knew we would not be bothered. Sometimes we drove to the top of the Horseshoe casino parking garage. Each new day began with immediate thoughts of where I could park that night.

Money consisted of the change I could find in pay telephones (yes, they still have those) or in the parking lots of major retail centers. There were days when I could only find enough to buy one taco for Paige. It became normal for me to buy two or three gallons of gas at a time and the fuel light stayed on continually. The one thing I could not do was let that car run out of gas. It was our shelter, our ark. If I ran out of gas on the side of the road there was no guarantee I could get some before a tow truck came along and hauled the car to an impound lot. If that happened it would all be over.

In late August the skies to the south began to darken and I noticed that the roadways coming into Shreveport/Bossier were packed with heavy traffic. I rarely played the car stereo and had no regular access to a television so I had no way of knowing that New Orleans was preparing for a hurricane. On August 23, 2005, Hurricane Katrina slammed into the Crescent City and wreaked devastation that is still evident ten years later. Suddenly, we weren't the only homeless people in Shreveport. Around the city temporary shelters sprang up to accommodate the influx of refugees. These stayed in place as Hurricane Rita followed on the heels of Katrina and barreled into Texas before swinging right up into Louisiana. I did what many parents would have done in my situation. I'm not particularly proud of it but if I had to do it again I probably would.

I lied.

I drove us to the shelter that had been set up at the Century Link Center in Bossier City and told the people there that we were from Houston and had been forced to evacuate our home. No questions were asked. We were given cots and hot meals. The only thing I can state in my defense is that the shelter never filled to capacity while we were there. No one was denied entry because of our presence.

The crisis passed and soon the shelter was closed down. We were back on the street again. It was September and the temperatures had cooled some. In the evenings I continued to read. There was something important about Thoreau's narrative I needed to understand but my mind was often distracted, my thoughts scattered. During the day we often found ourselves back at the racetrack cheering for Jeff. The truth is that a part of me had given up and was just waiting for the inevitable to happen. As things turned out, the inevitable was right around the corner.

Louisiana Downs was preparing to host the Super Derby as September was winding down. The Super Derby at that time carried a purse of one million dollars and attracted some of the best horses in the nation. Jeff had invited us to attend the event with his family. He was certain that he would have few horses to ride on Super Derby day; the top trainers preferred to bring in top tier riders such as Calvin Borel and Mike Smith to pilot their horses. Jeff decided we would all enjoy the event together from the clubhouse. I was hesitant because we had no fancy clothes to wear. When I saw the look on my Paige's face, however, I knew I couldn't say no. Somehow I would find a way to wash our best clothes before race day.

The next day an amazing thing happened. After the races Jeff invited us to his home. This had never happened before and I was floored. Homeless and hanging out with a professional jockey. It was all very surreal. When my daughter and I arrived at the Burningham home we were greeted by Jeff who seemed to be in a fit of excitement.

"You won't believe this," he told me. "I just got a mount for the Super Derby!"

It wasn't that hard for me to believe. Jeff was one of the most talented riders on the circuit.

"Which horse?" I wanted to know.

"Military Major."

My jaw dropped. I was at the racetrack often enough to know the horse…and his owner. Military Major was owned by George Steinbrenner. The horse had been very successful in lower-level stakes races and it appeared that the owner of the New York Yankees was ready to try his horse against tougher competition.

Jeff wanted to know if Paige would be willing to babysit his daughter, Larissa, that evening so that he and Lacie could attend a pre-race party. I was asked to stay also. The situation was becoming more unbelievable by the minute.

I agreed, of course, and the Burninghams went off to celebrate. Those few hours in Jeff's home were like an oasis in the desert. It was cool inside, there was food to eat, and television. For the first time in a long while I was able to relax. When Jeff and Lacie came in that night I was asleep on the couch in their living room and Paige and Larissa were asleep upstairs. I woke up and Jeff told me to stay put and spend the night.

We were the guests of Jeff and Lacie the next day at the Super Derby. When Jeff won a race on the undercard that day he invited us both to stand with him in the Winner's Circle while a picture was made with the winning horse. In the main event Jeff guided Military Major to a fourth-place finish despite being given little chance by the oddsmakers to do well against some very nice horses. After the race Jeff and Lacie took us to dinner at a very nice restaurant and then asked us to spend another night at their home.

The next morning as we prepared to leave Jeff stated that the meet was ending at Louisiana Downs and he wanted to stay in touch. He was on his way to Miami for another stakes race but said he was planning on taking Larissa to Six Flags over Texas when he returned. He wanted us to meet them there. With no idea how I was going to get the money for gas I agreed. We still had the season passes I had purchased earlier that year and maybe it was time for me to go back to Texas. Asking Jeff to help me find work wasn't something I could bring myself to do.

The next time I saw Jeff Burningham my daughter was gone and so was the pride that came before my greatest fall.

9 DESPERATION

I sat in the parking lot of a brand new Wal-Mart in Arlington, Texas and considered a course of action that was in no way reflective of the person I always envisioned myself to be.

My family wasn't perfect by any means. It was, in fact, quite dysfunctional. Nevertheless, I'd grown up with a clear understanding of right and wrong. Most of this can be attributed to my grandmother. If there is indeed such a place as heaven, she is there. She was never preachy about her faith but it was a part of who she was. My grandmother...or "Granny" as she was called by her children and grandchildren alike...lived her life by a simple principle: treat others as you would want others to treat you.

She imparted moral lessons in very unique ways. Most of the time they involved stories from her own life experience. One of my favorites involved my grandfather and a house fire.

When my grandmother was a young wife with several children (she had eight all told) my grandfather left their small farmstead to look for additional work in the neighboring fields. Granny was left at home and tasked with minding the children in addition to tending the crops. While my grandfather was gone a fire broke out on the property that threatened to consume everything the family owned. Granny was forced to fight the fire with only the aid of her older children while trying to keep two toddlers safe. In spite of the odds Granny managed to put out the fire.

Later that evening as she said her nightly prayers, Granny made a very specific request.

"God," she prayed, "if we ever have another fire please let my husband be home."

My grandfather returned home and a few weeks later fell asleep in the bed with a lit cigarette. The mattress quickly caught on fire. Granny was forced to put the fire out as well as tend to the badly burned hands of her husband.

The moral of this story, Granny said, was to be careful what you pray for.

Sitting in that Wal-Mart parking lot I prayed for the first time in many years. I asked God for it to end. Not my life, but the struggle we were facing every day. We had spent the previous ten days in the Dallas area waiting for the day we were supposed to meet Jeff and his family at Six Flags. Now, every penny I had was gone and the gas tank was on fumes. Neither of us had eaten in several days. What had I done by agreeing to come here? Why couldn't I have just told Jeff the truth?

My perspective was gone. I knew what I was about to do was wrong. I wasn't even making an attempt to justify it, not to myself or to anyone else. Desperation had me in its clutches and was squeezing the life out of me like an anaconda. When I did manage to get a breath it only served for the beast to tighten its grip.

I did bargain with myself, though.

Just this once, okay? No more. We are meeting Jeff soon and I will tell him everything and ask for his help. Everything will be okay.

I told my daughter that we were going to stop at the store to get out of the car for a bit and just look around. Once we were inside I allowed her to venture off on her own while I carried out my dirty work.

Up and down the food aisles I went with a buggy, pretending to shop for groceries but actually singling out anything I could fit into my pockets. The weather was cooler so the jacket I wore did not seem out of place. Whenever I encountered an aisle that was clear I would pretend to read the label on a can of tuna while slipping another can into my jacket. Small things like Vienna sausages and potted meat were my targets. My daughter had to eat something. Anything.

Perhaps a half-hour later we met up and I said it was time for us to go. As I made my way to the exit doors I thought I saw some familiar faces. There were a couple of people it seemed I had seen on several aisles standing by the exit doors with shopping bags in hand. I briefly considered the possibility that they were loss prevention employees waiting for me to leave the store but dismissed my thoughts as paranoia. These were just shoppers. Seeing them several times was just a coincidence.

My heartbeat escalated as I walked casually toward the door.

Everything that happened immediately after I made it outside is a blur. The sound of running feet. Angry voices. A firm hand on my arm.

A tall young man, one of the people I had seen at various times, turned me around and began to march me back inside the store. I was horrified to see that a young female also had my daughter by the arm and was pushing her forward. Both of us were taken to a windowless room in the store where the items I had taken were inventoried and totaled. I had taken just shy of fifty dollars in foodstuffs. The young man informed me that the police had been called.

Paige was in hysterics. I tried to calm her down and tell her everything was going to be okay. The young man explained to me that I was lucky the total had not exceeded fifty dollars. That would have made it a more serious crime. As things were, he said, I'd probably be given a citation and allowed to leave with a warning never to enter Wal-Mart again.

An officer from the Arlington Police Department came into the room and briefly conferred with the loss prevention team. He asked me for my identification and I gave it to him. The officer stepped outside for a few moments. When he came back in he asked me to accompany him outside. Paige wanted to come also but he assured her I would be fine and instructed her to stay put.

Once we were outside the officer asked me about the incident. I was completely honest with him. I confessed to taking the items and gave him a short version of everything that had happened in the past few months. He seemed genuinely sympathetic. I was allowed to go back to Paige and sit with her for a few more minutes before he once again called me outside.

"I don't like to arrest parents in front of their children," the officer said, and then he told me to place my hands behind my back.

As he produced a pair of handcuffs and secured them on my wrists he told me that a check I had written in our last days in Tyler had bounced and a warrant had been issued. Not only was I being arrested for the bad check it was his decision whether to issue me a ticket or take me to jail for the shoplifting. He had chosen the second option. I protested and begged and asked him why. He told me he believed it was in Paige's best interest. My circumstances necessitated that she be placed with someone else until I could properly care for her.

The officer was right, but that didn't stop the intense pain I felt as he drove away from that Wal-Mart with me in the back seat of a police cruiser. This time my cries weren't silent. They were the sobs of a man that was completely broken, a man that had lost the last thing in his life that meant something.

I was booked into the county jail on a misdemeanor theft charge and placed in a cell to await a court hearing. That night, looking out at the city through a small window that was covered with wire mesh, I wondered where Paige was. Had she eaten? Had she taken a bath? Was there a bed for her to sleep in? Were the people caring for her nice to her? There was so much I wanted to know, and so much I wanted to say to her.

I never even got to say goodbye.

PART TWO:
MY CONSCIOUS ENDEAVOR

"I know of no greater fact than the unquestionable ability of a man to
elevate himself by a conscious endeavor."
Henry David Thoreau, *Walden*

10 SIMPLIFY

Within a few days of my incarceration I was assigned a public defender and scheduled to appear in court on charges of misdemeanor theft. I spoke with the attorney once and he handled our brief interview like a shepherd handles sheep. He told me that my case was cut and dried, a done deal. I would plead guilty and be given the maximum sentence—thirty days in jail. I had no qualms about this. I was guilty. The time I served would also apply to the bad check.

There is something I want to say here before proceeding with my story. I never once saw myself as a hero, not even after everything I went on to accomplish after these difficult times. At best I am a flawed individual. The theft was a minor mark on the complex tapestry that is me but it should serve to reinforce the understanding that I am human and subject to the same capacity for error as anyone else. This book could have easily been written by glossing over this episode but it would rendered these pages an equivocal account of my journey.

Someone in the sheriff's department was able to provide me with the information I wanted the most: where was Paige? In the immediate aftermath of my arrest she was taken to the home of a distant relative that lived in the DFW metroplex. After that arrangements were made to return her to the custody of her mother in Minnesota. It was also made clear to me that the person responsible for the abuse that had placed her in my care was no longer in the home.

Was there terrible sadness at losing her? Of course there was, but there was also a sense of relief. She would have a bed to sleep in and food to eat. She would return to school and be able to catch up on the work she had missed since the new school year started. My daughter was going to be okay. No matter how dark my personal clouds were I had to take comfort in that. The arresting officer had genuinely done both my daughter and myself a favor.

The men in my cellblock were all in jail for similar, minor offenses. At least one of them had been arrested for vagrancy. Vagrancy is just a fancy legal word for being homeless. He was a double amputee and confined to a wheelchair. We got to know one another and shared our stories. It was good to commiserate with someone that understood the pain I was in. Sometimes we shared food that we'd been given by other inmates that had money to purchase items from the commissary. I will never say that my time in jail was good, but I will say that it wasn't as bad as what I perceived jail to be. I had a bed and three meals a day. There was cable television and hot showers. In short, it was a world better than how I had been living.

During the day inmates were allowed to congregate in a large dayroom. At night we had to return to a private cell that was locked. I often went to my cell early to read something from the jail library. I had tried to locate a copy of Thoreau's book to no avail but I did find a Bible and some other literary classics. When the lights went out I would think about the things I had read. My mind always kept coming back to Thoreau, though, and his trip to the Maine woods. I began the process of trying to break down his experience piece by piece and look for principles that I might be able to implement in my own renewal. The quote about making a conscious endeavor resonated. What was Thoreau trying to say?

New Age wisdom has become very popular in this day and age. Everywhere you look someone in promoting positive thinking as a means of repairing your life. I find much of that stuff to be very cliché and not a very honest approach to life. Aren't we being dishonest when we try to put a positive spin on everything that happens? If I cut my finger with a knife am I supposed to say, "Behold, I have slashed it for my benefit!" with a goofy grin on my face? I heard Tony Robbins sum up my feelings on the "fluffy bunny" New Age movement in a powerful way. If you go out to your garden, Tony explains, and stand there repeating *there are no weeds*, does that remove the weeds from the garden? Of course not. It takes more than positive thinking to enact real change.

The thing that appealed to me about Thoreau was the practicality of his approach. He defined a personal philosophy and then set about getting his hands dirty while implementing it. He didn't just talk about making a conscious endeavor. Thoreau actually made one and *Walden* was his record of it.

I started thinking about the quote and the entire book and slowly began to formulate an outline of what it meant to make a conscious endeavor. What comprised the power behind the words? In my way of thinking there were three parts.

The first key to making a conscious endeavor was waking up.

Consciousness implies being awake. Awake means that we are aware of our surroundings and circumstances and are moving through life with intent, with purpose. I couldn't help but see how waking up also demanded taking personal responsibility for what my life had become. For the first time I was able to honestly look at my past and own the mistakes that had contributed to my downfall without making justifications. Thoreau was extremely dissatisfied with his own life and the lives of other men when he had his awakening, but that awakening produced in him a profound honesty to recognize his own flaws and shortcomings. He saw his life clearly for the first time.

You will never be all that you can be until you learn to recognize everything you aren't.

When it came to pursuing my dream of a writing career I was lazy. I had no work ethic. In some ways that laziness even manifested itself in my deep affection for a job that had required hours of mindless driving from place to place. I had not challenged myself to be anything beyond a man that could scrape by, and look at how that worked out.

The second principle I discovered to making a conscious endeavor was *building equity.* When Thoreau went to the woods he carried a hammer and some other tools. From the first day he began to invest himself mentally and physically in recreating his life. He didn't wait for someone to come along and build him a cabin. He envisioned the cabin he wanted, cut down some trees, and went to work.

There is a great program in America called Habitat for Humanity which helps people achieve home ownership by actually building them a home. A condition of receiving this assistance is that the new homeowners must put in a required amount of "sweat equity" or physical labor in building the home. It doesn't matter what their skill set is. They don't have to be carpenters. They can paint, plant shrubs, or even clean up the pieces of lumber that are dropped. What Habitat for Humanity has learned is that when people invest in creating something they appreciate it more.

Building equity in myself was something I had not done. I had not invested time in becoming a better writer so I could have that writing career. I had not invested money by setting aside a portion of my earnings, no matter how small, for my future. I had not invested in furthering my education and thereby making myself more marketable and reducing the risk of extended unemployment.

Building equity in yourself also speaks to value and self-worth. *Others will never become invested in you until you become invested in yourself.*

The third concept I uncovered while contemplating Thoreau's work was this: *an elevated life is not static.*

Once Thoreau finished his time beside Walden Pond he returned to a more civilized form of living. *Walden* would become his most celebrated literary work but Thoreau continued to write on a variety of subjects that ranged from civil disobedience to how seeds are naturally distributed to populate forests. He never stopped growing and evolving. Thoreau continually challenged his mind and his visions of an ideal life.

Evolution is nature's law. Species that do not evolve are doomed. I was starting to understand how crucial it was to keep refining my vision of success in order to keep growing. In my time at the taxi company I was inert. I went to work and collected a check and ran like a hamster on a wheel. I wasn't growing. It was becoming clear to me that a successful and fulfilling life was one that was always moving in the direction of some purpose.

If you stop growing, you stop living.

Days passed while I meditated on the life of Thoreau and waited for my day in court. The life I'd been living just a few months ago felt like a distant memory. I was all for forgetting it. I didn't think anything about those months could be a cause for joy.

Until the jailer brought around the mail one evening and placed a letter from Jeff and Lacie Burningham in my hand.

11 THE LONELIEST BAYOU

I sat on the bed in my little cell and cried like a baby. Jeff and Lacie had been worried when I did not meet them at the amusement park and had begun an effort to track down my whereabouts. The two of them managed to piece together many of the events that had led me to homelessness and then began calling law enforcement agencies to inquire after me. That's how they found out about my arrest.

They both chided me about not asking for help. They would have helped me find work, they said. I knew it was true. They had also gained some information about Paige and had spoken to her. It was so wonderful to hear from them that she was okay. The letter concluded with a promise to stay in touch and be there for me when I was released.

On my twentieth day of incarceration I was called to court and given a sentence of time served. I was a free man. I wasted no time in contacting Jeff and Lacie. This time I wasn't going to let my pride stand in the way of asking for help. Now I didn't even have a car to give me shelter. I needed someone. I needed them.

Most people dream of leaving their hometown to find something better. I would also imagine that for most of these it remains a dream. I'd often thought about leaving Texas but the circumstances of my departure weren't something I'd imagined. Here I was riding down the I-20 corridor with every possession I owned in a few bags. I had no family, no money, no car, and no job.

Instead of thinking about all the things I lacked I tried to focus on what I had. My health was good. My mind was sharp. Jeff and Lacie had gone out of their way to demonstrate that they cared about me by offering to help me get back on my feet. They wanted to give me a place to stay and assist me in finding work. Lacie picked me up and off I went to the Burningham Farm in Louisiana.

There is a joke they tell in Louisiana that goes like this: what is the loneliest bayou in the world?

Bayou Self.

My inherent nature had always been to weather the slings and arrows of life alone. I was the only child of a mother that didn't do a great job of showing affection. In school I had very few close friends. I learned over time to laugh alone and cry alone. I can remember living with my grandmother and retreating to my bedroom when people would come over to visit. Some of them remarked to my grandmother that this was strange and that I must have some kind of problem, most likely drugs. The truth is that I was a loner. It's all I knew how to be.

During my failed marriage I had to have my space. If I was in our bedroom reading or watching television or trying to write I was apt to get upset if my wife came in. The only person that ever really broke down my walls was Paige. We could spend hours together and I never felt the urge to distance myself from her.

The unfortunate byproduct of my character was an inability to ask for help when things went bad. Pride is a double-edged sword. There is nothing wrong with taking satisfaction in being self-sufficient. Sometimes, though, even the strongest among us need to be lifted up when we fall. I had reached a place of humility about my state, a place of honesty. I was acting on the things I had learned from Thoreau.

The first step in making a conscious endeavor is waking up.

Consciousness means being honest with yourself about where you are and where you want to be. I had to face the fact that I needed help no matter how painful that was. I needed to resolve that repairing my life was going to take a lot of work and that I might need help for a while. The only way to start designing the life I wanted was to take an honest look at the one I had and accept what it would take to fix it.

Jeff and Lacie had a nice farm just on the outskirts of Shreveport. When we arrived it was turning cold and Jeff was riding at Delta Downs in Vinton, Louisiana. Lacie told me that on his next day off he would be coming to the farm to pick me up. I would return to Vinton with Jeff where he believed I could find work on the racetrack.

My experience with horses was very limited. Jeff knew this but he had many contacts in the racing industry. I was sitting in the track kitchen one morning when Jeff called and told me to meet him in one of the barns. I made my way there and Jeff introduced me to one of the most successful trainers on the Louisiana circuit, Brian House. Over the years Jeff had ridden many of Brian's horses. The two of them had done well together.

Brian needed an extra hotwalker in his stable. On the racetrack hotwalkers are the entry level, bottom of the barrel workers. When a horse returns from training on the track in the morning the hotwalker must "cool" the horse out by hand walking it around the barn. Many trainers only have their horses walked a few rounds before giving them a bath and putting them on a mechanical walking wheel. In the Brian House barn it was not uncommon for a hotwalker to walk a horse for 45 minutes, especially after a race. Brian offered me the job at a salary of $250 per week. I felt like I had won the lottery.

I'd been staying with Jeff in his swanky RV but my job with Brian necessitated living on the racetrack. I was given a 12' x 12' concrete tack room as my living quarters. Lacie Burningham found me a bed and drove three-and-a-half hours to bring it to the track. She also brought me a microwave oven so I could prepare TV dinners in my room. Whenever I opened the door of my room I was standing in the shedrow of the barn. More than once a horse kicked my door as it was being walked around. One night about three a.m. I heard the unmistakable sound of galloping hooves outside my door. A horse had broken free of his stall and was making circles around the barn. There was never a dull moment living on the track.

I'd only been working there for a few weeks when Brian called me into his office. He told me that he was very proud of my work and that I had become a valuable member of the team. He wanted to promote me to the position of groom and gave me a raise in pay.

Even though I didn't show it I was terrified. Grooms are responsible for almost every aspect of a thoroughbred's care. They clean the stalls, wrap a horse's legs with bandages when necessary, and brush the horse every day. Additionally, a groom leads the horse to the paddock when it is in a race and stands with the horse for a picture if the horse wins. Of all the people working in a thoroughbred barn the groom spends the most time with a horse each day. It was a huge responsibility, one I wasn't sure that I was ready for.

Brian House had spotted something in my work ethic that made him think I could handle it. He took a lot of my training on himself, spending hours with me explaining the reasons behind why certain things were done to maintain a horse's health and happiness. I thrived in my new position and learned a great deal.

Jeff and I remained close, of course, and we often spent our days off together. Jeff had a friend named David Elston. David was also a jockey. The three of us hung out often and were great friends. One day Jeff talked to me about the possibility of becoming a jockey agent.

Jockey agents are licensed sports agents that are tasked with finding horses for their jockeys to ride in a race. An agent can be crucial to a jockey's success or failure. They must know how to handicap a race and spot horses that are potential winners. Jeff's agent was Rob Robertson, one of the best on the circuit. Rob was pretty new to the agent business but he had a keen sense of how to spot good horses and get Jeff on them.

I was intrigued by the idea but knew nothing about the job. Rob offered to help me learn. In order to become an agent I would first have to pass a licensing exam administered by a steward at the racetrack. Everything was happening so fast but I soon found out that Jeff had a plan all along. David Elston needed an agent. In Louisiana jockey agents are only permitted to have two riders and David was being helped by Rob in a non-official sense. David wasn't the most talented rider on the track but Jeff and Rob were convinced that if I worked hard the two of us could make a decent living.

After my workday was over in the barn I would study the racing manual to prepare for my test. As the meet at Delta Downs neared an end I approached the head steward Julian Dupuis about taking my test and obtaining a license.

When I went in to speak to Mr. Dupuis he was very rude. He told me that he was not giving any licensing tests this late in the meet and that I would have to wait until racing began at Louisiana Downs to take my test. He then added insult to injury by informing me that there was a $5 fee to take the test.

"Do you *have* five dollars?" he asked me as I stood in his office.

I wanted to tell him that just a few months prior to that day I had nothing, but that today I had money and something even more valuable: I had a new awareness of how important it is for a man to have a purpose that will drive him through any obstacle that appears in his path. I wanted to elevate myself to a great height and nothing was going to stop me from doing that. With a smile I excused myself and began preparing to take my test at Louisiana Downs.

I came back to Shreveport with Jeff and David a couple of weeks before the meet began. As soon as the stewards arrived I made my way to the racing office to request a test.

When I knocked on the door of the steward's office and was admitted my heart caught in my throat. Sitting behind the chief steward's desk was someone I recognized immediately. The man sitting behind that desk was a racing legend.

Bill Hartack still holds the record for the most Kentucky Derby wins with five. He rode some of the greatest horses in history including Northern Dancer and Majestic Prince. He looked up at me from behind the desk and waited for me to speak. I wasn't sure I was going to be able to find my voice.

"I'd like to take the agent's test," I stammered.

Bill Hartack told me to sit down while he asked me about my experience on the track. I didn't have very much to speak of. He listened intently and then spoke to me about the qualities of a good agent. Finally, he reached into his desk and took out a copy of the exam. I was taken to a private room and allowed to begin. Mr. Hartack came by several times to check on me while I took the test, and one time even gave me the answer to a particularly hard question while explaining it to me. I finished the test and handed it in and was sent out into the racing office to wait as Hartack graded my work. About ten minutes later he called me back in to his office.

"You blew the test out of the water," Hartack said and smiled. "You only missed a couple. Come over here and let me explain why you got them wrong."

Hartack went over the test in detail and gave me further advice on being an agent. He concluded by telling me I could call on him anytime for help.

At one point during my time at Louisiana Downs I asked Bill Hartack which of his five Kentucky Derby victories was the sweetest and he replied without hesitation that it the year he rode Iron Liege.

"Why?" I wanted to know.

"Because that was the one I wasn't supposed to win."

You'll never accomplish great things if you listen to the people who say you can't do it. When someone says you can't do something, get excited. You have an opportunity to prove them wrong. When someone says no one has ever done it before, rejoice. That just means you'll be the first one to do it. A lot of people told me I didn't have enough racing experience to be a jockey agent, that my jockey was a poor rider and that we would not get any horses to ride, and many other reasons why I couldn't succeed.

Your success is your responsibility. It depends on you and your desire, not on what others think you can or cannot accomplish.

12 BUCKING THE ODDS

David Elston and I began our first racing season at Louisiana Downs in Bossier City with limited opportunities for success. David was still relatively unknown to trainers and I was in my first meet as an agent. One of the veteran agents on the circuit told me one morning that David would be lucky if he rode sixty horses during the whole meet. If that was the case both David and I were in trouble. Jockeys are paid a token fee, usually in the neighborhood of $50, for each horse they ride that does not finish first, second, or third. If they finish in the top three their earnings are a percentage of the purse money an owner receives. Agents typically make as much as twenty percent of what their clients earn from each race but I was a new agent and had agreed to help David out by cutting my fee to a ridiculously low percentage. The only way either of us could make a living was for David to ride a lot of horses and get lucky on a few of them. He simply did not have the credentials to secure rides on the top horses.

I questioned myself a few times in those first days at the track. My job with Brian House had been secure and I could have remained with him and earned a meager living. The problem was that I would soon be back in that cycle of dependency on my job. Even worse, my job as a groom would also be dependent on staying healthy. Grooming racehorses can be a dangerous business. If I got hurt I would be right back in the same boat I'd been working hard to climb out of. I was indeed waking up to the reality of what I wanted my life to be and grooming racehorses was a stepping stone not a destination.

My approach to being an agent was simple. I got to the track early each morning, between five-thirty and six, and began to systematically walk through each barn on the backside. Actually, I didn't walk. As Lacie Burningham stated once, I *stormed*. I was a man on a mission. I would ask trainers if they had any horses that needed to be worked out. Sometimes they said yes. Most of the time they said no. I just kept attacking those barns, knowing that every horse David was allowed to get on in the morning was a potential race entry in the afternoon.

Since I was allowed to have two riders I had also taken on the "book" of veteran rider John LeJeune. John had been on the Louisiana circuit for years. Both his father and younger brother were jockeys. There was a time when John did pretty well but he was getting older and his opportunities and skill had diminished. John came to me one morning with a list of trainers he had ridden for in the past. Beside each name was a phone number. He told me this was a good place to start looking for horses to ride.

The first name on the list was Sharon Soileau. I immediately called the number provided and my call was answered by a woman that sounded like she was busy working. She was out of breath and I could hear horses whinnying in the background. I introduced myself to Sharon and told her I was a new agent representing John and David. We would be happy to ride her horses, I said, and I hoped that she would give us a shot.

To my surprise Sharon was overjoyed! She told me that she had some horses that would be running soon and would be happy to let my guys ride some. I couldn't believe my good fortune. This was way too easy. It wasn't something I knew right then but Sharon was probably just as happy to have an agent calling.

Sharon Soileau grew up riding on the legendary bush tracks of Louisiana where horses competed in head-to-head, unsanctioned races organized by their owners. It was a brutal circuit with few rules. Owners sought out young kids to ride, some as young as nine or ten, because they were small. Some were so small that an owner would have to tie them to the saddle to prevent them from falling off. Many of horseracing's top jockeys—Calvin Borel, Kent Desormeaux, and Randy Romero to name a few—began their careers on those same bush tracks. In Louisiana, horse racing was and remains a part of Cajun culture.

By the time she graduated from high school Sharon was on the way to becoming a professional jockey. She obtained her license and rode a few horses but opportunities for female riders at that time were slim. It was also common for female jockeys to suffer sexual harassment from trainers that wanted favors in exchange for the chance to ride their horses. Sharon would never give in to these demands and often quit working for a trainer in disgust when she found out what he really wanted. Her career as a jockey was prematurely ended when she suffered a severe injury while exercising a horse one morning. The horse broke both of its front legs at a full gallop and Sharon was driven into the ground breaking her collarbone. To this day she still suffers from neck and back pain.

There is a stubbornness about Sharon that often manifests in a refusal to accept defeat and she found another way to participate in the sport she loves by becoming a licensed trainer. The very first horse she saddled as a trainer won its race and Sharon was off to a successful start that continued for several years. Her horses consistently finished in the money—first, second, or third. Her stable blossomed and grew. Horseracing stables, however, tend to experience success in cycles just like an NFL or NBA team. Successful horses get older and must be replaced by "rookies" that need time to grow and mature. When I met Sharon she was in a cycle of rebuilding her stable. Her stats had dropped and she had not registered a win in many months. She had one owner that had supplied her with a group of horses that had been mishandled by their previous trainer.

In short, we were a basement-dwelling football team. Sharon was the coach, I was the offensive coordinator, David and John were the quarterbacks, and the horses were the blood and guts running backs that were trying to take us to a winning season. It was a daunting scenario for all of us.

Some of the horses Sharon had were talented, though, and under her care they started to show some promise. The most spectacular of these was Bobbyn Bouie, a gray gelding that had racked up a series of uninspiring finishes. In his most recent outs before my riders took the reins he had failed to even finish a race. On one of the first times he entered the paddock for a race after I became an agent his odds were more than 100-1. In an effort to help him focus Sharon had added blinkers and a set of black earmuffs to drown out the crowd noise. He came strutting into the paddock looking like Batman and I felt like the Joker.

Bobbyn Bouie started to improve, though, and things really took off when I picked up veteran female rider Lucy Burch. Lucy took over the primary riding duties for Sharon's stable and pretty soon the horses were finishing in the money again. Everything was going great until tragedy struck. Lucy was killed in a car accident that left all of us reeling. Sharon took it especially hard. Somehow we were able to pull ourselves together and soldier on.

Sharon and I worked closely that summer at Louisiana Downs and our relationship began to deepen. I finally summoned up the courage to ask Sharon out on a date. She initially refused, stating that she would need to think about it. I learned later that when I asked her she had been casually dating someone else and refused to begin a new dating relationship while that was still in progress. It wasn't going anywhere, though, and Sharon broke it off as soon as I asked her out. She messaged me to say she accepted and actually offered to cook me dinner at her place.

When I arrived at Sharon's home I was reminded of the farm I'd lived on with my stepfather, the man my mother drove away with her alcoholism. Ironically, Sharon had ended up on her farm after her previous marriage collapsed due to her husband's alcoholism and physical abuse. She'd bought the place with an old friend from high school. Together they became partners in Thunder Run Ranch and this was where Sharon stabled and trained all of her horses. The centerpiece of the farm was a huge pole barn with more than 12 horse stalls. When I inquired about it Sharon told me that she had built it herself with the exception of putting in the massive poles that were too big to manage alone. The feat took her six months.

I was starting to see someone that maybe knew a thing or two about making a conscious endeavor. Sharon was a fighter. She'd been through her share of hardships and had managed to build a successful business in spite of them all.

Given all the things that had happened to me I wasn't sure just how far the relationship would go. We really hit it off, though. As the meet drew to a close at Louisiana Downs it was clear that we enjoyed being together. Little by little our relationship became more serious. I was headed off to Delta Downs again for the winter but Sharon would be running her horses there often. Right before I left she told me that she wanted me to come and live at the farm when the meet was over.

As things turned out David Elston rode more than 60 horses during my rookie season as an agent. 200 more, in fact. I had done what I set out to do and had found someone I cared about. Sharon's stable had starting doing well again. Even Bobbyn Bouie went on to earn over $50,000 in purse money. I thought about each of us and realized that we were all bucking the odds. Life had given us a few knocks and I am quite sure there were many people that thought we wouldn't get up. We all did. That group of people and horses is one I will never forget because all of them are wonderful examples of persistence and the pursuit of a goal.

For the first time in almost two years I had a sense that the clouds were starting to break.

13 PAYING THE PRICE

Everything I had been doing since moving to Louisiana was accomplishing the second principle of a conscious endeavor. I was building equity in myself. Every horse stall I cleaned, every moment I spent studying to be a jockey agent, and all the work I had done to represent my clients at the track was an investment of hard work that made me feel as though I was an active creator in my recovery.

I moved to the farm and was able to devote time to helping Sharon with the physical chores. The peacefulness of my surroundings started to stir something in my soul, a long abandoned flame that was waiting for the slightest puff of air to get itself going.

I wanted to start writing again.

There was an unused building on the property right next to the main house that had been the residence of Sharon's uncle when he was forced to evacuate New Orleans during Hurricane Katrina. Sharon told me that I could use the building as a place to write. She had also given me a computer as a gift. In just about everything I've wanted to do Sharon has been a source of encouragement.

In the early mornings and late afternoons I would retreat to the building to write. Sharon never disturbed me. It's as if she understood how much I needed and savored my solitude. My earliest efforts weren't that good. My initial efforts were at creating short fiction but I wrote many things during that time. All that mattered was to keep writing. At long last I was taking Joe Lansdale's advice. I was building equity in myself as a writer.

I was paying the price.

About once a month I would take a trip into the city to play poker at the Horseshoe casino and it was on one of these trips that I came across a free copy of *Ante Up Magazine*. They gave issues away in poker rooms all over the United States. *Ante Up* covered the poker scene and featured stories on professional and amateur players. It was a nice monthly read. I've enjoyed the game of poker since I was first introduced to it at the ripe old age of seven. That's kinda what happens when you have a barfly for a mom. You get exposed to a lot of vices.

In 2010 I noticed an ad in *Ante Up* that said the publishers were looking for something they called an "ambassador." The ambassador for a specific region would be responsible for gathering news from their local poker rooms and writing an article for the magazine once a month. I began to think about it and thought to myself, why not? I could write and I knew the game well enough. At the very least it would be an opportunity for me to build some more equity in my writing skills. Once I got home I fired off an application to the editor and waited for a response. I tried not to get my hopes up; surely there were hundreds of applicants.

A few weeks later I got an email from Chris Cosenza, one of the founders of the magazine and its current editor. He was very interested in having me become an ambassador for the magazine and hired me right away. "Hired" is not precisely accurate. The job offered no monetary compensation. What it did have was a monthly column with a byline, and I was determined to make the most of that by sending in my best work.

I didn't know any of the big name poker professionals. It was a big industry with numerous shows on television that had turned people like Phil Hellmuth and Daniel Negreanu into overnight celebrities. Annie Duke had even parlayed her poker career into a stint on Donald Trump's *Celebrity Apprentice* where her feud with Joan Rivers became legendary. I was only required to cover the local poker rooms in Louisiana but I wanted to make a splash. With no contact information I turned to the Yellow Pages of the digital world—Facebook.

Several poker professionals had Facebook accounts but few of them had fan pages. I started sending friend requests to their personal pages and many of them accepted. One day I was very pleased to see that Jerry Yang, the WSOP World Champion in 2007, had added me as a friend. As I became familiar with Jerry's own story I really wanted to do some kind of piece on him as an extra assignment to demonstrate my worth as a writer. I messaged Jerry and told him I was a writer for *Ante Up* and would like to interview him. Within minutes Jerry had messaged me back to say he would be very happy to do it.

We arranged a time and Jerry called me on the phone. For the next hour we spoke about Jerry's own upbringing in Laos where he and other children would often take the bladder from a butchered pig and inflate it so they could have a ball to play with. He had watched other children he knew starve to death and die from disease before his parents decided to try and immigrate to the United States. Jerry told me how they crossed a river in the dead of night with bullets flying over their heads. All around them people screamed as they were hit.

The family made it and started their own conscious endeavor to make a new life. Jerry and his siblings went to school and grew up to attend college. After graduation Jerry embarked on his own successful business ventures. It was after winning a WSOP seat in an online poker tournament that Jerry became a household name. With scarcely more than a year's worth of playing experience under his belt Jerry bested more than 6,000 other players to claim the crown of world champion at the World Series of Poker Main Event in Las Vegas. Jerry collected millions for his win and promptly made good on a promise to donate ten percent of his winnings to charity. He also used the money to launch a new restaurant named after the hand that won him the WSOP title—Pocket 8's.

Listening to Jerry's story was inspiring and it sort of put my own troubles in perspective. Here was a guy that had been shot at as a child and been forced to craft toys from the carcasses of dead animals. He had suffered racial slurs when his family came to America. They had been forced to live in some of the most dangerous slums in the United States while his parents worked to put their children through school. I've said it before and I'll say it again: life is this amazing well of inspiration if only we are willing to drink.

Chris Cosenza was so happy with my interview and the subsequent work that I submitted to *Ante Up* that he called me one day with some wonderful news.

"We want to pay you for your column," he said.

I think I was speechless for several moments. A paid column in a nationally-published magazine. Was I the same guy that had been living in a car just a short time before? How did I get here from there? The answer was that I had been making that conscious endeavor, first by waking up and then by building equity in myself. Thoreau was right. It was possible for anyone to elevate themselves.

My column appeared each month in 2011. I was sent all over the state to cover poker tournaments and was able to meet lots of interesting people. At the same time I had begun to build a business of my own developing web content for bloggers and website owners. The business did so well that I resigned my jockey agent's license and began working full-time from the farm.

I was on top of the world until I awoke one fine spring morning with flu symptoms and a smudge in my field of vision.

Life wasn't done knocking me down yet.

14 MULTIPLE SCLEROSIS

When I was very young, perhaps five or six, my mother had noticed that I often stumbled. She took me to the doctor about this and he ordered that I wear a set of braces not unlike those worn by the fictional character Forrest Gump. I was forced to wear them only for a short time and then the doctor pronounced me well. That was good enough for my mother but I continued to stumble well into my teens and adulthood. It was ultimately chalked up to being uncoordinated and clumsy.

One morning in the spring of 2012 I woke up with what felt like flu symptoms. I was feverish and sore. What concerned me most, however, was a smudge in the field of vision of my right eye. It was like looking through a lens that someone had left a greasy thumbprint on. The flu symptoms didn't bother me much but the vision problems were concerning. My work demanded that I spend long hours at the computer. If there was something happening with my vision I wanted to have it treated right away.

I made an appointment with an optometrist in our little town. It was clear when I arrived that he did little more than write eyeglass prescriptions. He examined me and dilated my eyes but was unable to explain the smudge. He referred me to Dr. Brian Vekovius, an eye surgeon in Shreveport.

Dr. Vekovius ordered a full workup on me and did a variety of tests. Once these were finished he examined me himself. After looking over all of the test results he turned to me with a somber expression.

"You are experiencing optic neuropathy. It's a serious condition that can be attributed to one of several underlying causes."

He explained to me the three things that could be causing my vision problems. The first was a tumor. Dr. Vekovius told me that he was 95% certain this was not the cause. The second was an infection. This had been ruled out because of my bloodwork and other tests.

"So, what is the third possibility?" I asked.

"I really think what we are looking at is Multiple Sclerosis."

When he said it a few images popped into my mind but the most vivid one was of an emaciated Richard Pryor in his final days of the disease. The once energetic comedian had been reduced to a mere husk by MS, a disease that attacks the myelin sheath that covers a person's nerves.

As Dr. Vekovius explained to me, the nerves in our bodies are a lot like electrical wires. The insulation that surrounds them is made of a substance called myelin. Imagine what would happen if you were using extension cords in your home that had no outer insulation and that those wires came into contact with other wires in the same state. The result would probably be throwing a breaker in your house when the wires made contact. MS is a little bit like that. When the myelin sheath deteriorates around the nerve cells they begin to fire erratically. This can cause pain and a disruption of the signals from the brain. This often manifests itself in stumbling.

When I told him about my stumbles as a child I was distressed to find out that a great number of MS cases go undiagnosed in children because the symptoms are often wrongly attributed to the clumsiness of a growing body.

As the disease progresses it leaves scar tissue, or lesions, in the brain. These lesions are detected by an MRI. Lesions can appear or not appear depending on whether or not the MS is in an active state.

I was sent to another physician and also ordered to see a neurologist. Over a period of time the picture became clearer and more symptoms emerged. I had advanced Multiple Sclerosis. The good news was that the optic neuropathy could be treated successfully. Other symptoms were just something I was going to have to live with.

One night I was sitting at home when it began to feel like someone was squeezing me around the chest area. I was worried but tried to convince myself that I had indigestion or something of that nature. When I went to bed, however, I could not breathe when I became prone. At that point I asked Sharon to drive me to the hospital. My fear was that I was having a heart attack.

The hospital doctors admitted me and explained that I was suffering what is known as an MS "hug" or Girdle Band Sensation. The hug is one of the most painful symptoms of MS. It feels like someone has a belt around your chest and is tightening it little by little until you have difficulty breathing. It was one of the most frightening experiences I've ever had.

In the immediate days after my diagnosis I became very depressed. There was also some small sense of bitterness about it all. I had worked so very hard to make my conscious endeavor and this seemed very unfair. I can remember thinking to myself on more than one occasion that perhaps Thoreau was just an idiot, a nutball that concocted some crazy plan to live like a hermit and then write about it. Maybe he was mentally ill. I had no way of knowing. How in the hell could he advocate the power of the human spirit? Tell my doctors about the human spirit and its ability to overcome obstacles and weather crisis, I railed. I tried your plan, Henry, and look what happened. The whole conscious endeavor thing was beginning to look like fluffy bunny nonsense.

I knew my feelings were just the product of dissatisfaction and depression over my illness, and I allowed myself to have them...for a time. As soon as I felt myself beginning to lose genuine perspective, however, I began to take a fresh look at Thoreau and the things I had learned. By now I had another copy of the book and I dove into it like it was my first time. As I read I thought about those nights in that small jail cell and the enlightenment I had been given. Suddenly, I realized I that I had not been following through on the third premise of making a conscious endeavor. My life had become static again.

After all of the things I had accomplished I had reached a point where I had stopped challenging myself with new goals. My depression really didn't have anything to do with the diagnosis of MS. I was just using the MS as a scapegoat for my own lack of motivation. It was far too easy for me to turn my disease into a crutch, an excuse for (to use a poker term) cashing in my chips and just resting on the progress I had made thus far. Well, I had been down that road before. I knew what happens when a man gets inert and loses purpose. I needed something to stoke the fires, something to renew my drive for personal excellence.

That something was delivered by the sweet voice of a lady named Terry Marlow.

15 LIFE CHANGING PHONE CALL

Something I had considered for a while was returning to college full time to obtain the college education that I had so foolishly passed up after my high school graduation. It was something I knew would renew my purpose and give me a sense of satisfaction, but knowing that still didn't keep me from procrastinating for a variety of reasons. I couldn't afford it. I didn't have time to spare. It was just a dream, I told myself, but at least I was dreaming about something positive.

I even signed up for a free class from the University of Michigan that was offered by a company called Coursera. Coursera was making news for its innovative approach to education. The company had partnered with several schools to provide free college level classes in an online format. There was no college credit given but participating in a class called Internet History, Technology, and Security made me feel like I was doing something to facilitate continued growth and development. I also filled out requests online for college degree programs.

As 2012 drew to a close I was happy with the progress I'd made in redeeming my life. Every year since 2005 had offered something to celebrate, some milestone that could be held up as evidence of my conscious endeavor. My life was once again assuming an even keel, but this time around I wouldn't allow myself to become passive and inert. There were still goals and new benchmarks to pursue.

The requests I had submitted to various online college programs were mostly forgotten until my mobile phone rang late one morning. It was New Year's Eve and I was going about the routine business of the farm. Things never stop on a farm, not for holidays or birthdays or anything else. There are always animals to feed and other chores to be done. I typically screen calls from a number I do not know by letting them go to voicemail but something compelled me to answer the phone.

"Hello, this is Terry Marlow from University Alliance calling on behalf of Florida Tech Online."

I was intrigued. Of all the requests for information I submitted Florida Tech was the only school to respond. I'm not sure why the other colleges didn't bother and it may not have mattered. In the time after submitting those requests I'd done a pretty good job of trying to convince myself I couldn't go back to school. I specifically had an idea that I would not qualify for the grants and student loans that would make school possible for me.

When I was writing my column for *Ante Up* and covering the world of professional poker I made an important observation. The most successful players on the circuit were the players that consistently bet on *themselves*, not the cards. The cards were of no consequence. It was the decisions and choices the players made that mattered and not one of them entertained doubt in their ability to win. No matter what obstacle they faced the great players never entertained the possibility of defeat. "A chip and a chair" was their motto. They believed that was all they needed to win.

I can imagine that Thoreau may have tried to talk himself out of moving to the woods. Was there a risk of failure? Of course there was. No enterprise comes without risk, but a key part of making a conscious endeavor is being willing to bet on yourself. That willingness is increased over time as we make good choices and establish a track record of working diligently with purpose, but we must summon it continually in order to elevate ourselves.

Terry began by asking me about my goals, not just in academics but in life. I appreciated that because it spoke to the concept of purpose. I told her that I wanted to be a good example for the grandchildren I had inherited as a result of my relationship with Sharon. I also wanted to rectify my greatest regret which was passing on the scholarship offered to me in high school. From a career standpoint I was pretty clear on my wheelhouse and what I wanted to do. Writing was my gift and profession. We discussed several programs and Terry explained to me the advantages of pursuing a psychology degree.

Wait a minute. Was I actually discussing this with Terry as if it were really going to happen? We needed to slow down a bit. All of this discussion was moot if I couldn't afford school.

"I don't think I can qualify for financial aid," I said. I really didn't want to lead Terry on when she could be assisting someone else that actually had a chance.

Without missing a beat Terry said, "Let's try anyway."

"I haven't been to school in so long that I'm afraid I will fail," was my next excuse.

"We're going to help you succeed," Terry said.

Next objection, please.

For about thirty minutes I reeled off a list of reasons why I couldn't go back to school. Terry answered all of them without delay. I am firmly convinced that Terry had no intention of letting me escape that day. By the time we finished talking I was actually enrolled in the next spring semester!

I was excited but my excitement soon turned into anxiety. What had I done? Granted, I had always had a tendency to make snap decisions but this was insane. It occurred to me more than once to call Terry back and tell her that I had made a mistake.

A few weeks later a box arrived from Bisk Education, the company that is heavily involved in facilitating online classes for many top universities. Inside the package was a welcome letter and a very nice school planner. There was also a mouse pad emblazoned with a panther and the Florida Tech logo. Something clicked in me right then and I started to believe that maybe, just maybe, I could do this. In a few more weeks I opened my email to find a notification from Florida Tech advising me to accept my financial aid package for the coming year. To my surprise I had qualified for a Pell Grant and would also be issued student loans to cover the cost of my tuition. It was all quite overwhelming.

At 45 years old I was officially a freshman at the Florida Institute of Technology.

PART THREE: CATCHING EXCELLENCE

"Gentlemen, we will chase perfection and we will chase it relentlessly, knowing all the while we can never attain it. But along the way we shall catch excellence."
Vince Lombardi

16 REAL LIFE LARRY CROWNE

Being a fan of comedic films it was hard for me to miss comparisons with some classic cinematic characters. Adam Sandler's Billy Madison was one. Rodney Dangerfield's Thornton Melon was another. The film that really struck home, however, was *Larry Crowne*. In the film Tom Hanks plays a middle-aged retail store employee that is dismissed from his job without warning and returns to college in the hopes of making himself fireproof. Along the way he learns a lot of things about himself and finds a true sense of purpose. Every time I watch that film now I relive all of my college memories and think about the winding road that put me in a degree program at Florida Tech.

Before classes started I was assigned a student advisor that would be tasked with guiding me through my entire academic journey. I was a little disappointed that Terry Marlow wouldn't be the person doing that but this is how things worked and Terry assured me that she was just an email or a phone call away if I ever needed anything. In the run up to the first day of class my new advisor called and introduced himself. We chatted for a brief period of time and he scheduled another call for the first week of classes.

Terry had sold me on a track in Applied Psychology. My initial thoughts were to pursue a degree in Liberal Arts. If you've been to college you will know that choosing a Liberal Arts track can be synonymous with *I have no idea what I want to do*. Terry wasn't going to let me off that easy. I made it clear to her that writing was my intended career path. Florida Tech did not offer an online English degree but their psychology programs came highly recommended. The school is one of those that meet the stringent requirements necessary to receive the American Psychological Association's stamp of approval. As Terry explained, pursuing an Applied Psychology degree would make me a better writer and expand my skills. She was correct. The volume of papers I prepared as a student at Florida Tech was staggering…and beneficial. My mechanical skills improved exponentially with each new paper submitted.

Finally, the first day of classes arrived. I was taking three of them: Introduction to Psychology, a basic skills computer class, and an orientation class that would familiarize me with Florida Tech and its online platform. I was told by my advisor that I must log in to my classes at least twice in the first week or I would be dropped. In my time zone I was actually able to get in to the platform at 11 p.m. on the night before classes began. I signed in and began to explore the platform.

One of the first things I wanted to do was find out a little bit more about my professors. I figured that this was a good way to evaluate the "seriousness" of the program. Before attending Florida Tech I had only participated in online learning via Coursera and my emotions there were somewhat mixed. My instructor at Coursera, Dr. Chuck Severance from the University of Michigan, was highly regarded and his lectures very informative. As a student, though, you never interacted with Dr. Chuck because there were more than 100,000 people taking the class. While I enjoyed Coursera I did find it at times to be less than stringent in terms of what I expected from a provider of college level courses.

In that very first phone call with Terry Marlow I asked some very specific questions. I wanted to know about the degree I would be earning. Was it a recognized degree? Would my diploma state that I had been a fully online student or would I receive the same one the students on campus received? Those kinds of things were important to me. Terry assured me that yes, my degree would be recognized and also be the same one I would have earned on campus. Even so, I still had some doubts about the quality of the education I was going to receive when I logged in that first night.

I noted the names of my professors and turned to that wonderful tool Google to see what information I could find. Right away I discovered that Dr. Stephanie Lopez, my psych professor, had published numerous journal articles and also worked for NASA. This rattled my cage a little bit. There was no scenario I could envision where a NASA scientist would reward an inferior effort. Things got real when I saw that.

The second thing I noticed was that there were about 30 students in my class. Not 100,000. It doesn't take a rocket scientist to understand that in a class of 100,000 a student can sort of disappear if their work ethic is poor. In a class of 30, not so much. I was going to have to work hard to distinguish myself as a serious student. Everything I did would be scrutinized by my instructors.

Let me say right here that before I started school I developed a mentality that I would go on to use in every class at Florida Tech. I basically began each new class with an attitude that conveyed my seriousness. I let my fellow classmates and professors know from day one that I would be the one setting the bar. There were a few occasions I was criticized for that by other students. They perceived it as an attempt to show off or ingratiate myself with my professors. It wasn't that. It was simply a desire to be the best I could be. Once when I had been a little roughed up over it Dr. Amy Green from UNLV told me that she had used the same approach in her academic career and to never apologize for this attitude. I felt much better about it after we talked.

The next morning my phone rang and one of my advisor's assistants was on the other end. He started by asking me if everything was okay.

"Yes. I mean, I think so."

"Well, the reason I ask is that our records show you have logged in 22 times since the classes opened a few hours ago. I don't think I have ever seen that before. I just wanted to make sure there wasn't some issue."

I assured him there was no issue whatsoever and explained that I was simply doing what I thought an online student should do. He complimented me on my enthusiasm and wished me well.

This will sound arrogant and it is not meant to be, but within the first couple of days I knew I could not only handle school but that I could excel. Everything in the online platform was crystal clear. I knew what was expected of me each week. The work was tough, but college was supposed to be challenging. This was just what I needed to satisfy the third requirement of a conscious endeavor. School was going to renew my purpose and help me to keep moving forward as I designed a better life.

With all the eagerness I could muster I plunged in.

17 BUMPS

My perception about you, dear reader, is that you are not naïve. It doesn't make sense to me that you would purchase a book like this if you were. So, if I told you that everything at Florida Tech was smooth sailing you would have some difficulty swallowing that. I believe that reasonable people understand that each path we follow in life has its share of bumps. It's how we respond to those bumps that matters.

There was some dissention brewing with my student advisor. It had started in one of our very first phone calls when I stated very clearly what my goal was as a student. I told him I was going for an A in every class.

"Gonna try to get honors, huh?" he responded, and then he did something that made me very angry.

He laughed.

It didn't seem like a good-natured laugh, either. To my ears it was mocking and I took offense. From that moment on we had a strained relationship.

The second issue was that my advisor routinely missed scheduled phone calls. Maybe this is not a big deal for many students but for me it was huge. I live on a farm and work with horses. Farms and mobile phones do not mix. They get dropped in water buckets or stepped on or clogged with dust. You learn very soon that phones need to remain in the house while you are out tending to chores. To be honest there is something I enjoy about being outside without worrying about taking calls. I explained this to my advisor and told him that as long as I knew the approximate time we would be speaking I could be certain to be in the house and take the call. After he missed two straight appointments that he had scheduled I was becoming stressed.

To be fair I want to say right here that I can see circumstances where my advisor was not at fault. Perhaps that laugh was just his personality and

I took it the wrong way. Or maybe he had been told that by so many students that didn't follow through that he had become a little bit jaded. Maybe he missed our appointments because he was talking to another student that needed some extra assistance. It is what it is and I hold no ill will towards the advisor. What I do know is that I simply needed the interaction and encouragement. I perceived myself as low maintenance but I still wanted that person there to motivate me and appear invested in my personal success. My first advisor just wasn't satisfying those requirements.

With no idea where to turn for help I reached out once more to Terry Marlow. Terry told me that even though she could not help me directly she would find someone that could. While I waited to hear back from someone I started to have some feeling that maybe my need wasn't such a big deal to the people at Florida Tech. After all, I was just one of hundreds of online students. Maybe I was just a number to the people that ran the online program.

Not long after I spoke to Terry I received a call from Dr. Stephani Cuddie, the manager of online COPLA (College of Psychology and Liberal Arts) programs at Florida Tech. She asked me about my situation and listened patiently as I explained my dilemma. When I was finished she responded to me and I could hear genuine concern in her voice.

"I want to handle this for you," she began, "because my concern is that if it isn't handled you will think about going to school somewhere else."

It was like the world around me stopped while those words just sort of hung in the air. Was I really that important to Florida Tech? Why would they care so much about the success of one student? After all, I was still doing well in my classes...all A's. It wasn't like helping me with this situation was going to change that (although I believe it could have in the long run).

The call was concluded with a promise from Dr. Cuddie that she would get me a new advisor. She told me that she knew just the person I needed.

I never told Dr. Cuddie this but when that call was over I walked outside to the little grove that Sharon and I had designed for the grandkids and sat down by myself. I looked around at my surroundings and realized for the first time in forever that there were people who cared about me. Genuinely cared. I was someone to the people at Florida Tech. I was someone to Sharon and the grandkids that called me Poppy and loved me like their own flesh and blood. I had taken the second principle of making a conscious endeavor, building equity in myself as a person, and now people were investing in me. Tears flowed openly down my face as I experienced the joy that came from knowing I wasn't alone.

My life mattered.

It was only an hour or so before the phone rang again.

"Hey, Scotty. My name is Tony Porrevecchio. I'm going to be your advisor at Florida Tech."

The rest, as they say, is history.

18 TONY AND ME

Tony Porrevecchio proved to be just what I needed at Florida Tech. A talented advisor can take a good student and make them into a great one. Tony did exactly that during our time together.

Tony called me each week to discuss my progress and talk to me about how my life was progressing outside of school. Whenever I felt down he was there to pick me up and give me the motivation I needed to continue. With every A I earned he was there to congratulate me, and when the dreaded college algebra dented my 4.0 he was there to console me.

Math has always been a difficult subject for me; I suspect this is the case for many college students. The only classes I did not earn an A in at Florida Tech were College Algebra and Statistics. After those classes Tony reinforced something that Dr. Stephanie Lopez had told me in my very first term. I didn't have to be perfect or earn the highest grade in all of my classes. I only needed to be the best I was capable of being.

My best was pretty good. I was repeatedly praised by my professors for the papers I turned in and my work ethic. I think that having Tony as my advisor helped me give my best each week, and he wasn't the only one. One of the last classes I had on the way to my Associate of Arts degree was a new offering titled Research and Computer Literacy. I believe I was a part of the inaugural class and was very happy to discover that Dr. Cuddie was going to be my professor.

Dr. Cuddie made it clear right away that she was going to demand my best effort each week. In one assignment she even offered some audio feedback in which she stated that while I was a student that she didn't have to worry too much about she was going to find things for me to improve on. Every assignment I submitted came with detailed instructions on how to improve even though I was already earning an A. Having a professor like that is like having a legendary coach to motivate you. It makes you want to work hard for them.

As the class was nearing a close some students voiced unhappiness in their discussion board posts about the grades they had received. I was compelled to send Dr. Cuddie an email in which I told her how thankful I was that she had challenged me as a student. I encouraged her to keep doing what she was doing because this was college and college was supposed to be a challenge. I ended the email with the quote from Vince Lombardi that began this section of my book:

"Gentlemen, we will chase perfection and we will chase it relentlessly, knowing all the while we can never attain it. But along the way we shall catch excellence."

The only way that you can ever create a life of value is by building equity and continually challenging yourself with new goals. Making a conscious endeavor is about raising the bar and pushing yourself to greater heights. Tony and Dr. Cuddie and pretty much everyone I came in contact with at Florida Tech understood this very well. They encouraged me to push the envelope and see what I was really capable of.

They helped me to catch excellence.

19 THE BLIP ON THE RADAR SCREEN OF ME

When I began my journey at Florida Tech I made a decision to keep my diagnosis of Multiple Sclerosis private. I did not want anyone to know because I didn't want to be treated differently from any other student. It was important for me to know that I did not receive any special consideration because of my illness.

There were times when MS made being a student very difficult. One of the biggest problems was a symptom known as spasticity which causes the muscles to cramp. During my time at Florida Tech I suffered debilitating spasticity that made it impossible for me to sit at my computer for more than fifteen minutes at a time. I would work for those fifteen minutes, take a break of an hour or even more until the spasms passed, and work for another fifteen minutes. When these symptoms were at their worst it would take me three days to complete a 250-word discussion board post. My assignments were always turned in on time.

The other problem was the optic neuropathy. It became worse the longer I stared at the computer screen. There were a couple of terms when I had limited vision in my right eye or no vision at all. I only had to ask for an extension on an assignment twice and both times I simply chalked my request up to an illness without being specific.

The disease was weighing on me, though. Would you be surprised to know that the number one cause of death among MS patients is suicide? The pain and discomfort become intense and are also mixed with severe depression, another symptom of MS. I was not immune to any of these things. I read an interview with Montel Williams once in which he described his own battle with the disease. Twice he contemplated ending his life but chose not to do so. Having MS can be a sad and lonely path to tread.

I'm not sure why many MS patients choose not to discuss their illness. For me I think it was because I thought talking about the disease would somehow give it greater power, and I also really was afraid of how others would begin to look at me. There are a lot of misconceptions about MS that can sometimes cause people to act in ways that make patients uncomfortable. For starters, many people think the disease is an imminent death sentence. It is not. It does not automatically confer an expiration date although it is progressive and complications often lead to death as the illness becomes advanced. Since MS is neurological many people equate that with impaired mental function. While MS does indeed impair mental processes such as short and long-term memory over time it does not reduce one's intelligence or the ability to reason and process information. You'd be surprised how many times I have been spoken to like a child by someone who finds out I have the disease or how many people express sympathy as though I am living on borrowed time.

Keeping things to yourself can ultimately lead to moments of profound loneliness, and that in turn can lead to depression. As I neared graduation at Florida Tech I suffered both of these and on the July 4th holiday of 2014 everything sort of crashed down on me. Up until that point no one knew about my diagnosis except Sharon and a couple of close friends. I needed someone to talk to and I turned to one of my former professors at Florida Tech that had become a good friend since I finished her class. Dr. Amy Green allowed me to vent and helped me realize that perhaps it was time to open up about my illness to others. It made sense to me. I had to consider that there were other MS patients that might benefit from my story.

The next day I sat down and wrote an article for my blog. It summed up how I felt about my disease:

MY ANSWER TO MULTIPLE SCLEROSIS

Dear MS,

You and I should have a talk, one that is long overdue. If you intend to be my constant companion for the rest of my life there are a few things you need to know. This is not a discussion. I will talk and you will listen. Contrary to what you may believe, I am still calling a fair amount of shots in our relationship.

I will not conceal our little affair any longer. For almost three years we have courted in the shadows. I've hidden you away like a mistress and tiptoed through a lot of awkward minefields. That stops today. Let's open our union to the scrutiny of others…others who may not know you as well as I do and others that know what it is like to share your company in moments of depressive darkness. We will give the world an opportunity to judge us both. It's fair, don't you think?

I was frightened when you first revealed yourself to me during a moment of physical weakness. It did not help matters that you announced your presence by the means of optic neuritis that left me with a blind spot in my right eye. It was sobering to realize that the body I have trusted for these 46 years was now vulnerable to your advances. In my naiveté I thought ignoring you was the answer. Even speaking your name became forbidden, but you were undeterred by my unwillingness to return the attention you lavished on me. My silent acceptance of our partnership was acceptable to you, I suppose, but you made a drastic error.

You allowed my silence to lull you to sleep.

While you have been routinely going about your business of trying to destroy my physical body, well…I've been busy, too. About 15 months ago I went back to school to earn my degree. It's too bad that you missed it because it was spectacular. On my way to earning that degree I managed to also earn academic recognition and membership in an honor society. Not bad, huh? I never told anyone at the Florida Institute of Technology about you. I did not want to allow even the slightest possibility that I would be treated any differently than any other student. I didn't want what I was doing to seem heroic; it is not. Heroic is reserved for single mothers who find the time to complete their degree while working full time and raising their children. Heroic is reserved for that student who began their journey with a limited reading ability and went on to graduate with a 3.0. You see, every time I encountered a story like that during my time at FIT it was never lost on me how fortunate and blessed I am.

It wasn't easy. There were entire terms when I had limited vision, sometimes in both eyes (it seems that damaging my right one wasn't satisfactory for you). Spasticity limited the time I was able to remain at my computer, making it difficult to complete tests and writing assignments. I persevered in silence.

I won.

I'm going forward, too, you know? This first degree was just a beginning. Sorry if you had other plans.

You almost caught on to some of the things I was doing behind your back last year, and even succeeded for a time in deterring me from my goals. Remember the exercise routine I started? The one you disrupted by causing me to stumble twice in a matter of weeks and damage my knee? Knees heal, my cruel friend. The only thing in life that doesn't heal is giving up. Giving up is permanent. I maintain myself with a regular schedule of exercise and have a far healthier diet today than I did when we first met.

Truthfully, I have some things to thank you for. Last year I committed myself to writing creatively again. On my desk this morning there is a rough draft of a very fine screenplay, pages of a story drawn partly from my own emotional journey. No, not the parts of the journey that include you. Other parts. Parts that really matter. And all those songs I've written…it just didn't seem right to orphan them to that great pile of unfinished projects. I chose a few of them and wrote a few more. That noise you hear in the evening is me dusting off my vocal chops and running scales on the guitar to regain the flexibility that you tried to steal from my fingers. Don't be sad. If any of these creative projects achieve any measure of recognition, you'll be right there with me. We're together in this, remember? Partners in creative crime.

I met people, too. Good people. At least one of them is directly responsible for this little letter today. What? Did you think I was just going to shut myself up from the world around me? I don't think I will do that if it is all the same to you...or even if it isn't. It turns out that a lot of people value my friendship and they have gone out of their way to bring joy and happiness into my experience. I think I will return the favor.

Let's wrap this up, because I know that you have a full schedule. Trying to break me down is hard work! Here's the skinny: you have an ability to exert some control over my body but you do not have an ability to exert control over me. At the end of the day whatever I accomplish will stand apart from your presence in my life. Those accomplishments will endure. You will simply be a blip on the radar screen of me. I am not defined by this dance with you, Multiple Sclerosis. Strengthened by it, maybe, but not defined. I won't tell you to go to hell or go away. Stick around if you must. Enjoy the ride. It's going to be a pretty good show.

Your errant companion,
Scotty R.

Once I had finished writing that blog article I felt as though a huge weight had been lifted from my shoulders. It was liberating to let everyone know about my illness, not because I expected them to treat me differently or feel sorry for me but because I wanted them to take inspiration from my journey.

The human spirit can triumph in the face of adversity. All of my psychology classes had served to help me further understand Thoreau's humanistic mindset, and today I believe that nothing can trump a conscious endeavor.

20 HONORS

Things were winding down at Florida Tech. I was only a few credits away from completing a great personal redemption and earning my Associate of Arts degree. My GPA was strong—3.8—and I was on top of the world as I embarked upon my final classes.

In the mailbox one day there was a letter from Brian Ehrlich at Florida Tech informing me that I could submit an application to be considered for some student awards. These letters were sent to all online students, I am sure, and at first I dismissed the idea of applying. As I thought more about it, though, submitting the application made perfect sense. Even if I wasn't chosen it was very cool to be able to say I was considered. Around that same time I also submitted an application for the Pearson Student Advisory Board and progressed to the semi-final round of interviews before being eliminated from consideration. I filled out my application and sent it in, not really thinking that I had done anything spectacular to distinguish myself from the other students at Florida Tech.

While I waited for a decision I also was invited to become a member of Psi Chi, the International Honor Society for Psychology, by Dr. Maria J. Lavooy from Florida Tech. This was an amazing honor and I valued it even more because Dr. Lavooy was also the president of Psi Chi at the time. It made me feel good to know that I was being a great ambassador for my school and all of the professors that had invested their time in helping me to succeed.

A phone call from Tony Porrevecchio brought some great news. Tony told me that he had spoken with Lisa Anne Gill at Florida Tech and that she had informed him I was going to receive some kind of award at the Spring Honors Convocation. He didn't know what the award was but the only thing I could think of was the application I had submitted. A few days later I received another letter from Brian Ehrlich in the mail informing me that I had been awarded a designation of Outstanding Sophomore for 2014. For a long time I just looked at that letter and ran my hands over the paper in disbelief.

The Psi Chi induction and honors ceremony were held on the same weekend in April but I could not attend in person. There was just too much to be done on the farm. I was able to watch a live stream of the honors presentation via the Internet and smiled when my name was called. I didn't know if I was the first fully online student to receive an award for Outstanding Sophomore but I was pretty sure I was the oldest. The Psi Chi induction was actually held on April 18 which would have been my mother's 76th birthday. Even though we never had the best relationship I still cling to a belief that she was pretty proud of me on that day. Not only had I become the first person in my immediate family to go to college, I'd also excelled.

Just a couple of months after that I submitted my final assignment as a sophomore at Florida Tech and waited for my last grades to post. They came through and it was official. I had earned a college degree.

It was my firm intention to attend the graduation ceremonies that December but an unfortunate circumstance prevented my participation. Sharon's mother had been diagnosed with late stage pancreatic cancer and we were caring for her around the clock. I learned to understand what it felt like again to have priorities, and if I had to do it all over again I would do it the same way. She needed us to be there in her final days and it was my honor to be by her side.

The disease ultimately took her in February of 2015. Before she passed I was able to tell her about receiving my diploma from Florida Tech and she was proud of me. She knew that her only daughter was with a man that was doing everything possible to be the best person he could be.

It was a sad time and I needed a spot of good news to cheer me up. It came and was delivered by the most unlikely of suspects—a fellow writer from Scotland.

21 RECOGNITION

I've said this before and I will say it once again. When I started my academic journey at the Florida Institute of Technology I never had an idea that my journey would become an inspiration to others. To be completely honest my enrollment in school was originally conceived as a purely selfish enterprise. I was doing it for me because I needed to do it for me. I'm not unhappy in the least that others have been encouraged by my story and I do feel that all of us have a responsibility to use what we accomplish to inspire and uplift and make the world a better place, but it would be dishonest to say it was about that from the very beginning.

That's why I found it a little bit overwhelming when Gary Sprott called from Bisk Education to tell me that Bisk and Florida Tech were interested in producing a video that would document my experiences as a student. They also wanted me to come to Florida and walk with the spring commencement class so that I could claim my diploma in person. I was thrilled by the generosity of Bisk and Florida Tech and accepted the offer immediately, in no small part because I was also going to be able to visit the Bisk offices and thank Terry Marlow and Tony Porrevecchio in person.

Sharon and I left Louisiana for Florida in May of 2015 with our grandson Bryson in tow. There was something wonderful about making that trip with him because he had been one of the reasons I told Terry Marlow I wanted to go back to school. I wanted Bryson to have an example. Neither of his parents chose to attend college and this was distressing to me. How can we expect young people to place a premium on higher education when we as adults don't lead the way? I'm a firm believer that education can cure many societal ills. It can remove prejudice and unite people from different cultures. It can help narrow the gap between those that have much and those that have little. Ignorance is the driving force behind things like intolerance, hate, poverty, and the continued lack of sustainable resources. The very future of mankind's existence rests in the minds of the young. I believe that. But, like one of Thoreau's seeds in the forest, some of that hope will be extinguished if we do not nurture a fondness for academics in our children.

I had not been to Florida since that band trip of so long ago and was looking forward to seeing the coast again. So many wonderful things have had their birth on those Atlantic shores, things like space exploration that actually inspired the founding of Florida Tech. I was looking forward to being able to expose Bryson to the campus in Melbourne and would be lying if I said I didn't hope that someday he would walk those grounds as a student. Whether he chooses to go there or to another school I just want him to give himself the chance to become something greater, to do amazing things.

We were welcomed in Florida with open arms and my four days there were filled with emotion. I was able to look Bisk employees in the face and thank them for the work they do to help people realize their college dreams. I was able to stand among many of my fellow Panthers at the Grad Bash celebration and meet many of the professors that shared their knowledge with me. Finally, I was able to take that walk across the stage in the Clemente Center and receive my diploma. Every moment of that trip was precious to me and a memory that I will hold close to my heart forever.

Gary Sprott asked me to compose a record of my thoughts during the trip and write a series of articles. The concluding chapters of this book are my graduation diary, originally published on my blog and presented here in a slightly edited form. It is my hope that they convey at least some sense of how overjoyed I was to make the trip to Melbourne.

A short time after we returned home a film crew from Bisk came down to the farm and spent a couple of days shooting footage. I can't tell you how many times during their visit that I wanted to pinch myself to see if all of this was real.

I don't imagine that Henry David Thoreau ever imagined that his words would inspire a poor boy from Louisiana to do some pretty amazing things, but I think the fact that they did speaks to my belief that the genuine value in any accomplishment is the impact it has on others.

PART FOUR: GRADUATION DIARY

22 A JOURNEY OF 2300 MILES

The journey of a thousand miles begins with a single step. Well, something like that. I'm going to co-opt Lao Tzu's famous words from the *Tao Te Ching* for my own purposes and amend them with all due apologies and respect. My journey is going to be 2,300 miles round trip, give or take, and I'm not walking. Lao Tzu didn't have the advantage of a Ford F-250 Super Duty.

As my wife Sharon and I leave our little farm in Coushatta, Louisiana for the East Coast and the Florida Institute of Technology campus in Melbourne, I am able to relate to Lao Tzu's words. This trip actually began back on New Year's Eve of 2012 with that proverbial first step. That was the day Terry Marlow from University Alliance called me on behalf of Florida Tech. I'm still not sure what compelled me to take a call on New Year's Eve. I'm a *leave a message at the tone* kinda guy, especially when my mind is occupied by thoughts of an impending celebration that involves food, drink, and the singing of a song no one knows the lyrics to. I did answer the phone, though, and that's when the wheels of this journey really began to turn.

Neither Terry nor I could've had any idea during that first phone call that we would be here today. Wait...scratch that. Terry strikes me as the kind of person that believes in the ability of every student she works with to do amazing things. It is hard for me to process the way my journey has been magnified over the past months but I get it. How I got here makes for a pretty good story.

Back in 2005 I lost almost everything I had when a job I held for several years ended without any notice. I was literally working one day and unemployed the next. Call it ill fortune or call it bad karma for turning down a full ride to the University of Texas when I was 18. The end result was that I soon found myself homeless, living in my Ford Taurus while I struggled to find work and rebuild my life. The lack of a college education and any marketable skills made it difficult for me to find a job that would pay the bills.

Life wasn't done throwing curve balls, either. When I woke up one morning in 2012 with a smudge in my field of vision, a trip to an eye surgeon revealed optic neuritis. That didn't sound too bad until the doctor explained to me that the condition was a complication of Multiple Sclerosis. Those were dark days for me. I became depressed and more than a little bitter. Had I really been such a bad person that I merited these constant setbacks? I guess you could say I was still looking to blame someone or something for my challenges.

Terry Marlow's phone call was life-changing, a much-needed breath of fresh air that reaffirmed a belief in my ability to succeed. I resisted and threw up every objection I could think of but Terry patiently countered them all and just refused to let me get away.

Thank God for Terry Marlow.

Now here I am about to leave my driveway and make a long trip across multiple states to receive a diploma during the FIT Spring Commencement ceremonies. There are many miles for me to reflect on this journey and how it has impacted my life. 2300 of them, in fact.

2300 miles that began with a single phone call.

23 CROSSING LINES AND REMOVING BOUNDARIES

One of the great things about making this trip to receive my degree from the Florida Institute of Technology in Melbourne, Florida is being able to share the journey with my grandson. Bryson is handling the onslaught of miles very well from his car seat, and he just got a little bit excited when we crossed the Florida state line. I'm not sure he even understands what that means, really, and that's a great thing about kids. They don't regard lines and boundaries like adults do. Bryson only understands that he is getting to see new sights and meet new people.

My experience as an online student at Florida Tech was a lot like that. I shared classes with students from all over the world. Many of my fellow classmates brought their own beautiful culture into my learning experience. I came to appreciate all of the things that make us unique and I gained a new awareness of just how much we all share. No matter where my classmates were from, each of them was on a quest for personal growth. Some were there to learn engineering skills that will benefit their communities. Some were working on business degrees and will go on to start companies that promote economic growth in their homeland. Still others were learning information technology skills that can further dismantle the borders between countries and create global awareness of the concerns we all share. All of them were there to become better people.

My belief is that the things people want from life are not subject to geographical considerations. People want an opportunity to advance themselves and provide a better life for the people they love. People want the respect and admiration of their peers. People want security and stability. Education can be a springboard to all of those things and more, and online education in particular can extend that springboard to a greater number of individuals.

The thing about online education that encourages me the most is that it has the potential to erase those imaginary lines in the sand that separate us from one another. The only difference between Bryson and the people he just spoke to at a Florida rest stop is a geographical boundary. I hope that someday he will also understand this on a global scale. Crossing lines and removing boundaries is the first step toward the worldwide cooperation and fellowship we sorely need.

Online education also challenges the way we think about how learning is accomplished. Every student I was privileged to study with wasn't afraid to step beyond the conventions of traditional education. Because of that, lines and boundaries are becoming harder to see.

24 THE IMPORTANCE OF FAMILY SUPPORT

We originally intended to drive the first leg of our trip in one shot. It was doable; Sharon once drove nonstop from our home to Columbus, Ohio so that one of her horses could compete in a race at Beulah Park. In my days working as a courier driver I pulled the rare 16 hour shift. Having Bryson with us changed things a little, though, and Sharon had a great idea that she shared with me before we left. Her brother has a home in Watercolor, Florida. Making a stop there would just about split the drive to Tampa.

There was more to Sharon's idea than just a stopover. When she told me about it I could tell that something was on her mind. She reminded me that tomorrow would have been her Mom's 77th birthday. Mom passed away from pancreatic cancer in February. Caring for Mom during her illness was the primary reason we could not attend graduation last December. Sharon explained that it would be meaningful if she could spend at least a portion of that day in the company of her family and I agreed.

As things turned out, Sharon's brother was overseas fulfilling his duties as a pilot for UPS. His wife was home, however, and she was sitting on the front porch when we drove up. Connie is a great cook and served us a fantastic New Orleans meal of red beans and rice. Our room was elegant and decked out in beach decor. Watercolor is a resort community, the kind of place Sharon and I never get to see, so we appreciated everything about settling down there for the night.

My thoughts in Watercolor turned to the importance of family support for any student regardless of their age. I think that support can be even more important for non-traditional students. Sharon was there for me every step of the way as I worked on earning my degree from the Florida Institute of Technology. She had to assume more farm and household chores, encourage me when I was overwhelmed by my studies, and put up with my grouchy moods when I didn't get enough sleep during finals. I wasn't the only one making sacrifices; Sharon made plenty of them. Through it all she never complained. Sharon understood what I was trying to do and why it was important for me to complete the task.

Families are an important resource for an online student because the journey gets a little lonely sometimes. The value of having someone there to offer encouragement and support cannot be overstated. I am very conscious of the role Sharon played in my success, so conscious that I regard all of my achievements at Florida Tech as things we both share. Her reward has been seeing me evolve into someone that is better prepared and equipped as a provider. There is a source of pride in knowing that your significant other is committed to living their best life and to helping you live yours.

Not so far off in the distance the sound of waves can be heard as they roll in from the Gulf and I am reminded of John Donne's words:

"No man is an island entire of itself; every man is a piece of the continent, a part of the main..."

I am but a part of a family, a family that will soon include all of my fellow graduates from Florida Tech.

25 THE ROAD

We did another long drive today, about ten hours, but we are finally settled at the Hilton Garden Inn near the Bisk offices in Tampa. The beautiful landscaping here is a welcome sight after two days of travel. Old oaks, some of them probably older than I am, cover the property and stand regally attired in Spanish moss. Even the birds are quiet and do not disturb the peace of this place with meaningless chatter.

Serene.

Life is so much about the road that brings us to a certain point. I'm taking a little time tonight to reflect on the winding path that led me to this moment. It wasn't easy. It began with homelessness and the pain that comes from feeling lost, from feeling like a failure. It coursed through doctors' offices and fear-filled nights of contemplation on the subject of why my body was betraying me. The path took me through the online classrooms of Florida Tech where I was asked to harness inner resources I never knew I had. The late night study sessions, the fatigue, the exhilaration that came with every A earned…all of these were steps on the path. There were times when I wondered if I would ever emerge into a place where I felt at peace with myself again. Still, I pushed forward, looking for that place of quiet calm.

Tonight, standing in the shadow of these old trees, a powerful realization sweeps over me with the same level of intensity evidenced by the coastal tide.

I wouldn't change one step of this journey.

There is a peace that comes when we learn to embrace challenges as opportunities for growth. I didn't always understand that. If my life had taken a different road perhaps I wouldn't be standing here tonight on the threshold of my greatest personal achievement as a graduate of the Florida Institute of Technology. There are things I am doing today that never would have been possible without those days of hunger and loneliness and living in my car. I know more about the resiliency of the human spirit than I ever would have without the burden of Multiple Sclerosis. My life is infinitely more filled with joy and appreciation of each moment than it could ever be without the presence of each pothole and bump in the road. For every hurdle, I am grateful.

Far on the other side of our obstacles there is a place where the evening sun filters through the trees and Spanish moss to illuminate us with an awareness of how every experience from the cradle to the grave combines to create the vivid colors that will adorn the canvasses of our lives. Those colors are what make us unique. When we come to accept this we realize that every life is a masterpiece that merits our best effort to live with passion and gratitude.

26 SWINGING THE HAMMER

In a couple of hours I will have an opportunity to do something few graduates of Florida Tech are able to do. I'm going to look at my enrollment advisor and student services representative and thank them for all they did to help me succeed. When I was discussing this trip with Gary Sprott of Bisk several weeks ago I told him that I couldn't make any promises about being able to maintain my composure when the moment came. My emotions are already starting to churn.

Terry Marlow and Tony Porrevecchio of University Alliance/Bisk Education were instrumental in every part of my academic journey. Terry managed my initial enrollment and Tony saw me through about 15 months of school with bi-weekly phone calls and walked me through the registration for each new term. I appreciated both of them even more after I completed my degree and transferred to another university. It has been my experience that Florida Tech student reps set a high standard and that other institutions would do well to model their example.

My reps invested in me not only as a student but as a person. I wasn't a number or a faceless entity to them. Both of them took time to get to know me and craft my student experience in a way that increased my chances of success. It might have been possible for Terry and Tony to just shuffle me through the system and leave me to my own devices (although I doubt it because that doesn't seem to be the Florida Tech way), but they didn't approach their jobs like that. Their caring was genuine and apparent at every stage of the process.

There is little doubt in my mind that online education must continue its advance through the ranks of traditional academics. We have reached a point in human history where the idea that education can only be delivered on a physical campus is untenable. The world has become too vast. In the late 1950's, Earl Long built bridges in Louisiana that are still in use today. Those bridges made it possible for poor rural families to connect with the cities where there were better jobs and better schools. Far more than simple structures of steel, those bridges were symbols of opportunity. What Bisk is doing today (and has been doing for many years) is not unlike what the Long brothers did in Louisiana.

Behind every bridge built is a man or woman swinging a hammer. The reps that serve the Florida Institute of Technology are bridge builders, plain and simple. The thing about building bridges is that it can often seem like tiring, thankless work. There are days when you can't help but wonder if you are really making a difference. Sometimes it helps to distill things down to their most rudimentary essence.

Celebrate the sound of the alarm clock each morning because it is another opportunity to swing the hammer.

27 MISSION CONTROL

Dr. Jerome P. Keuper founded Brevard Engineering College, the school that would become the Florida Institute of Technology, in 1958 to provide continuing education opportunities for the "missile men" that were working at Cape Canaveral for NASA. FIT's long-standing tradition of excellence in education on the Space Coast continues today. My very first psychology professor at Florida Tech was also a NASA employee. Every Panther should take pride in the history and former students of their school.

Being armed with the appropriate knowledge of and respect for Florida Tech's history should have prepared me for my visit this morning to the offices of Bisk Education. For all practical purposes these offices are Mission Control for FIT's online programs.

Gary Sprott from Bisk picked me up from the Hilton Garden Inn and we made the short drive to the complex where I was greeted by many members of the Bisk family. One nice young woman had even decorated her cubicle with a welcome message for me. I can't imagine how Armstrong, Aldrin, and Collins felt when they returned from their legendary voyage but I imagine this was about as close as I can come. I was received with warmth and appreciation.

It was an awesome morning. I met with my student reps, Terry and Tony, and sat down for chats with the CEO of Bisk and other executives. Mike Bisk, the company's president, spoke with me at length. So many wonderful people–Shawn Daugherty, Maria Lang, Amanda Molinaro, and many more–gave this poor boy from Louisiana the royal treatment. The experience was one I will never forget.

As we finished filming, Shawn Daugherty asked me if I would be willing to speak to the enrollment reps before I went back to the hotel. It was my privilege to honor that request. What I really wanted was for all of them to know was how important they are to Bisk and the thousands of students that have passed this way. At times it was hard for me to hold back tears.

My life was changed in that little room where the enrollment reps work.

In the mid 1990's I visited NASA's Mission Control at the Johnson Space Center in Texas. I remember thinking how many people it took to put a man in space and how so many of the people that worked in that room did so in relative anonymity to the astronauts they guided safely to the lunar surface and back home again. You could make a strong argument that the real heroes sat behind those desks in Mission Control. I would also bet that every astronaut agrees with that argument.

So it is with the Bisk family. These men and women are the spokes that turn the wheel of online education. I hope all of them know that every step I take across the stage in Melbourne two days from now was made possible by their hard work and dedication. All of them will be walking with me on that day because I carry them in my heart and in the deepest part of my soul.

28 GRAD BASH

The GPS on my Android revealed that it would take about 15 minutes to make the drive from the Crowne Plaza Oceanfront to the Florida Institute of Technology campus, a good deal because I needed a few minutes to relax and take everything in after the whirlwind of the past week. I was about to see my school for the first time.

Our route took us through a residential neighborhood. That was probably a routing error but I am glad it happened. Melbourne has a close-knit feel about it. I understand that locals never perceive their city the same way that visitors do, but I think this is the kind of place where you'll probably run into someone you know at the A&W Root Beer joint or the Home Depot. That kind of atmosphere is well-suited to Florida Tech because the online student community was a lot like that. I shared several classes with a few students and made some great new friends. At the same time the location of the physical campus is a little ironic because FIT has such a global presence through its online programs.

Shawn Daugherty and Brian Ehrlich, the Assistant Vice President and Director of Online Learning, were waiting for me in a parking area just off the main entrance to the campus. Both took the time to share a little of Florida Tech's history and Shawn accompanied me on a walkabout. The photos on the Florida Tech website don't do the campus justice. The Botanical Garden is amazing. Dent Smith, the founder of the Palm Society, inspired the garden's collection of palm trees. All in all there are over 200 different species of palm, bamboo, and other rare botanical specimens. My only regret was that I didn't have more time to explore the garden.

A visit to the statue of Dr. Jerome P. Keuper is a must for any student that makes the drive to Melbourne. With an initial donation of $0.37, Keuper pursued his dream of higher education on the Space Coast and left behind a legacy of persistence and commitment to a vision. I took a few moments at the statue to consider how Dr. Keuper's dream helped to make mine a reality.

We made our way over to a huge tent where graduates and their families were mingling with one another and enjoying great food and free beer. I don't think I was ever happier during my trip than I was at Grad Bash. Each time I turned around there were smiling faces to greet me and shake my hand. I met so many of the people that were influential to my academic career. Lisa Anne Gill was there, and so was Julie Shankle. Dr. Mary Beth Kenkel, the Dean of the College of Psychology and Liberal Arts, stole me away for a few minutes so that I could meet Dr. Maria J. Lavooy, the Program Chair of Applied Psychology for online students and President of Psi Chi. Dr. Lavooy told me that I was one of the first online students at FIT to be inducted into Psi Chi, and I told her how terrified I was when being considered for membership. No Louisianan could ignore the similarity of her name with that of Marie Laveau. Dr. Lavooy thought this was hilarious. She later came over and talked with Sharon about her horses. I really can't overstate how wonderful everyone was and how great it was to get to know them as real people.

Then it happened. I saw Brian Ehrlich moving my way. The gentleman beside him was unmistakable. His face was the first face I ever associated with Florida Tech. Dr. Anthony J. Catanese, the President of the Florida Institute of Technology, came over to personally welcome me to the campus. We visited for a few moments and then I experienced one of the best moments of my life.

Dr. Catanese shook my hand and said, "I'm proud of you, man."

There is so much more I could say about attending Grad Bash and visiting the FIT campus, but what I really want to say to everyone currently attending Florida Tech Online is this: make the trip to Melbourne to receive your degree. Go to Grad Bash and walk through the Botanical Garden. Sit in the shadow of Dr. Keuper's statue and soak in all the history of this great school—*your* school. I promise you that your Panther Pride will swell and you will be keenly aware of the magnitude of your accomplishment.

29 COMMENCEMENT

Is this really happening to me? Everywhere I look on this beautiful Friday morning there are young people moving about dressed in caps and gowns. Many of the young women have decorated their mortar board with various exclamations: *Class of 2015! Panther Pride! Hire Me!* Young men walk by…all types, from pen-protected geeks to hulking football jocks. There is a buzz of happy conversation that dissolves into a gigantic hum of emotions.

At this moment I can't help but spare a few thoughts of how I came to be standing on the FIT campus awaiting the commencement ceremony, but only a few. I am far more consumed by what this all means to me right now, in the present. There is a passing sense of sadness. It feels like the end of my time as a Panther. Then it dawns on me that the very word *commencement* has nothing to do with endings. The best years of my life are beginning right now. My walk across the stage in the Clemente Center is literally a walk into a future filled with so many opportunities that seemed out of reach just a few years ago.

This isn't a chance, it's a *certainty*.

My goal at FIT was to give my best effort. College education is a partnership and that is the student end of the bargain. I was given some sage advice by my very first FIT professor, Dr. Stephanie Lopez. "Realize that you don't have to be perfect or the best in your class" she said. "Strive instead to make a perfect effort." Her words are on my mind this morning while I watch my fellow graduates pass by. Each of us chased perfection. We all caught excellence.

* * * * * * *

I checked in and then had to ask for assistance in finding my seat in the little auditorium where we all would wait to walk over. Brian Ehrlich did not miss the opportunity to ease my nervousness with a joke. "It's a test," he said. "If you can't find your seat you can't walk." Someone was kind enough to point it out and I found myself sitting next to a lady who was also an online student. She actually lived in Melbourne but her children and work obligations made it difficult to attend a physical campus. We talked about our journeys and they were very similar. When Bino Campanini, the executive director of FIT's alumni association, gave a humorous speech to the assembled graduates (Campanini shamelessly requested that we give him a standing ovation during the commencement ceremony), it hit me for the first time that I could rightfully claim to be a college graduate. Even better, I had inherited a whole new family as a Florida Tech alumnus.

We made the walk over to the Clemente Center through a line of professors on both sides of our procession. They applauded as we walked through. How can any life experience top what I felt at that moment? As we entered the Clemente Center, "Pomp and Circumstance" was emanating from speakers overhead. My eyes misted over as I thought back to my high school graduation, the last time I'd heard the music. I thought about my old band teacher who arranged a full ride for me at the University of Texas and how I turned it down, citing as my reason that I didn't want to commit my weekends to performing at football games. How disappointed he must have been then. I took comfort in knowing how proud he would be today.

An inescapable part of life is regret, and I am not immune. I have my share. Nevertheless, as I sat there listening to Dr. Catanese mention me in his commencement address I became powerfully conscious of how regret is not an excuse for the choices we make today. It doesn't matter how old you are—40, 50, 60—nothing is over as long as *you* aren't over. It all comes down to what you resolve yourself to do and what you are willing to do in order to make it happen.

As I ascended the steps of the graduation stage and received my first college degree at the age of 47, my faith in Henry David Thoreau's words…the words that have become my personal motto…was reaffirmed:

"I know of no more encouraging fact than the unquestionable ability of a man to elevate his life by a conscious endeavor."

As my Graduation Diary comes to a close I encourage you to think on a few things. Are you making a conscious endeavor to live your best life? What are you chasing? The fulfillment that you seek can never be obtained by leading what Thoreau called a "life of quiet desperation." Genuine empowerment comes from the realization that you are awake and able to take the actions that will direct your life toward a goal, a purpose. Finding purpose is what enables us to live a meaningful life.

CONCLUSION

I began this book by discussing how important it is for a person to understand that their chances to create a valuable life are finite. I am very aware that as I write these words MS is doing what it will do and working to limit my opportunities. Someday my disease will claim its final victory, but not today. It cannot rob me of this moment and in this moment I can make a conscious endeavor to do great things. I'm at peace with my disability because it does not have the power to define me or the legacy I leave behind.

As I was wrapping up the final edits of this book I awoke one morning to find a voicemail from my friend Will Vaughan. Truthfully, I consider Will to be nothing less than my own blood, a brother. For the past few years Will and his beautiful wife Christy have been there for me and uplifted me with encouragement and support. I love them both immeasurably. I listened to Will's message and could not stop the tears from welling in my eyes:

"Hey, brother. I just wanted to call you and tell you that I love you and thank you for everything you've ever done for me, and let you know that I am very appreciative of our friendship and our brotherhood. I cherish you and everything we have."

I don't know what Methuselah must have done to be remembered for 969 years, but I'm pretty sure the endurance of his memory was connected to how his life impacted the life of others. When I listened to Will's message I started to really understand what it means to mark the world with your presence.

The degree I earned from Florida Tech is a wonderful thing. I display it on my wall with pride. The certificate for my induction into Psi Chi and the award I received for Outstanding Sophomore at FIT hang there beside my diploma and I am always filled with happiness when I see them. There will come a time, however, when those pieces of paper will fade and deteriorate to nothing. All that will remain is a memory of my accomplishments. The value in anything you do is not measured by a piece of paper. It is measured by how it inspired others to make their own conscious endeavor and elevate themselves to a greater quality of life.

When the moment comes for me to exit this world I hope that my farewell service is a little different from my mom's. I hope that a chapel is filled with people that can say I helped them in some way to believe in their ability to overcome obstacles and succeed. I hope that they smile and laugh and recall things I may have said or done that brought them joy. Somewhere I will be smiling and laughing, too, and taking comfort in knowing that many of them will teach their children and grandchildren the power of a conscious endeavor.

Don't count on that happening anytime soon, though. I'm not through creating my legacy just yet. I'm still here and still giving MS a fight to remember. Every moment is another chance to do something fantastic, every day another golden opportunity.

Life can be a lot like trying to break a big boulder with a ballpeen hammer. Every day you get to take one swing at the rock. On some days you will break a piece of it, on others you'll just scar it. There will be days when you hit the rock and experience a jarring reverberation that vibrates to the depths of your soul when the hammer just bounces off and the rock escapes unscathed. On a very few glorious days you're going to hit the sweet spot and destroy a big chunk of your obstacle. No matter what the result is from day to day, remember one very important thing.

Every day that you wake up is another chance to swing the hammer.

Swing for the fences. I'm rooting for you.

ABOUT THE AUTHOR

Scotty Rushing continues to make his conscious endeavor today through his writing and efforts to spread awareness about the potential of online education. He is currently focused on creative writing and has several projects in the works.

Made in the USA
Middletown, DE
27 November 2015